"I wholeheartedly recommend to you. This book is like a life difficulties of raising daughters in ... ... will help you and your girls live free from insecurity."

from the foreword by **Jennifer Dukes Lee**,
mom of two teenage daughters and author of *It's All
Under Control*, *The Happiness Dare*, and *Love Idol*

"*Confident Moms, Confident Daughters* is the book my mom and I needed thirty years ago, as she battled her own body image issues and I was hospitalized for an eating disorder. The Confident Daughter Discussion Questions have sparked such nurturing conversations with my adult daughter, and the Confident Mom Challenges are both fun and healing. Thank you, Maria, for re-mothering the insecure little-girl part of this mom's heart and for giving hope that it is never too late to live free in Christ!"

Cheri Gregory, coauthor with Amy Carroll of *Exhale:
Lose Who You're Not, Love Who You Are, Live Your One Life Well*

"When I was growing up, I *never* felt confident in how I looked. My mom, bless her heart, would pinch the fat on my back just under my bra, reminding me I wasn't thin enough. She thought she was helping; she never knew that all it accomplished was to cause me to doubt I would ever be thin enough, pretty enough, or good enough to please her. Thank God mothering has changed since the late '50s and '60s! If you're the mom of a girl, you will appreciate the sound biblical wisdom and practical life applications (not to mention great prayers) in Maria Furlough's new book, *Confident Moms, Confident Daughters*. With honesty, clarity, and transparency, Maria shares her journey raising a daughter in today's world. Social media and all the images young girls face every day can easily cause them to compare themselves to others and lose confidence in who God has created them to be. Let Maria's sound words help you navigate raising a God-centered girl in a self-centered world."

Kate Battistelli, author of *Growing Great Kids*
and *The God Dare* and mom to Grammy
Award–winning artist Francesca Battistelli

"This book is a compelling invitation to become the kind of women we dream our daughters will be—confident and content, secure and free.

With humility and wisdom, Maria shows us how to surrender our insecurities and take hold of the confidence that is ours in Christ so that our daughters can do the same. Packed with practical tools and powerful application, *Confident Moms, Confident Daughters* is a lavish gift for any woman who wants to raise a girl who can look in the mirror and smile at what she sees. As a mom of three daughters and a mentor of many more, I'll be returning to these pages again and again."

Alicia Bruxvoort, mom of five and member
of the Proverbs 31 Ministries writing team

"In *Confident Moms, Confident Daughters*, Maria Furlough invites women to step into a new story of courage that radically redefines beauty and encourages our next generation of young women to rise up in godly strength, embrace a biblically accurate perspective of self, and pursue Christ-centered confidence."

Gwen Smith, host of the *Graceologie* podcast, author
of *I Want It All* and *Broken into Beautiful*,
and cofounder of Girlfriends in God

"In *Confident Moms, Confident Daughters*, Maria reminds us that moms must live in transparent, healthy, and life-giving ways if we desire to raise girls who lean more on truth than on toxic mindsets and wayward cultural beliefs. I appreciate her honest portrayal of her own life and how she helps set us free from our past and nudges us toward a beautiful future as moms, daughters, and most importantly, daughters of God."

Amanda Bacon, mom of eight, author of *Shiny Things:
Mothering on Purpose in a World of Distractions*,
and cohost of the *All the Mom Things* podcast

"*Confident Moms, Confident Daughters* is a much-needed resource for all of us in our journey to raise confident daughters. How can we lead them if we aren't living it out ourselves? Maria tackles the issues of self-image, true beauty, and self-talk while we feel as though we are drinking coffee with her in real time. You will laugh, shed some tears, and gain confidence in what true beauty really is—in fact, it's already yours to have!"

Lori Benham, wife of author and speaker
David Benham and mom of four

Confident
Moms,
Confident
Daughters

Confident Moms, Confident Daughters

Helping Your Daughter Live Free from Insecurity and **LOVE HOW SHE LOOKS**

Maria Furlough

Revell

a division of Baker Publishing Group
Grand Rapids, Michigan

Published by Revell
a division of Baker Publishing Group
PO Box 6287, Grand Rapids, MI 49516-6287
www.revellbooks.com

Printed in the United States of America

Library of Congress Cataloging-in-Publication Data is on file at the Library of Congress, Washington, DC.

ISBN 978-0-8007-3521-0

19 20 21 22 23 24 25   7 6 5 4 3 2 1

To my daughter, Faith—
This book was born when you were.
You made Mommy want to find a way
to fight for godly confidence.

To every young woman who has come to me
through the years with their struggles—
I prayed for you, I cried for you, and I
had to write this book for you.

Contents

Foreword by Jennifer Dukes Lee   11

1. Showing Her Confident   15
2. Naming Your Story   27
3. If We Don't, Then Who Will?   37
4. Mirror, Mirror on the Wall   57
5. A Moment on the Lips   77
6. Let's Get Physical   93
7. Sticks and Stones   107
8. On the Cover of a Magazine   123
9. Helping Her *Love* How She Looks   137
10. Our Jesus and Our Joy   155
11. Beauty from Ashes: My Mom's Perspective   171
12. Letters from Our Daughters   185

Confident Moms, Confident Daughters
   Manifesto   197
Acknowledgments   199
Notes   203

Foreword

I once went forty days without looking in a mirror. Yes, I actually covered all the mirrors in our house. By day two of my forty-day mirror fast, my husband had successfully negotiated small gaps at the sides of mirrors so he could see himself. But I went mirror-free.

I didn't thoroughly consider the implications of this mirrorless experiment before it began. You see, during those forty days, I had more speaking engagements than I'd ever had before because of the release of my first book. I stepped onto stage after stage without having a clue how awful my hair looked. (I've since seen the photographs. Yes, it was bad, and I likely left the audience with the impression that a small, woodland creature had found a new home atop my head.)

I underwent this mirror fast because, as a woman who had struggled through a lifetime of insecurity, I wanted to see myself through only God's eyes. But there was another, more pressing motivation: I wanted to model confidence for my two daughters. Lessons, as they say, are often caught, not taught.

My mirror fast was a protest against the self-degradation that we engage in as women. We tell ourselves that we're not enough—or we let our bathroom scales tell us that we're too much.

I was tired of how we, as girls and women, often see ourselves and each other as a series of parts and "thigh gaps," or lack thereof. Here's a heartbreaking fact: girls begin to fret over their curves even before they begin to learn cursive.

I was tired of the photoshopping and the airbrushing, and yet I knew I was guilty. (I have deftly wielded Instagram filters to magically take five years off my face.)

I was tired of being a hypocrite in front of my daughters. They were old enough to know when I was talking a good game and when I was actually living what I believe. I wanted to demonstrate what it means to walk confidently in God's unconditional love.

So when Maria asked me if I would be willing to write the foreword for a book about raising confident daughters, I couldn't type my all-caps YES fast enough. This is exactly the kind of resource that moms like you and me need.

I know Maria. She is a friend, a prayer partner, and a woman who writes every word to draw her readers closer to Christ. She is an honest, trustworthy guide, and knowing that, I wholeheartedly recommend *Confident Moms, Confident Daughters* to you. This book is like a life preserver for any mom drowning in the difficulties of raising daughters in an image-obsessed world. These pages will help you and your girls live free from insecurity.

Think of this book as a way to metaphorically cover your own mirrors so you and your daughters can see yourselves through God's eyes.

When I participated in my mirror fast, I covered the mirrors with paper. Written on those pieces of paper were words such as *beloved*, *chosen*, *enough*, *beautiful*, *approved*. Every morning, as I stood at the bathroom sink, my eyes scanned the words on those papers, and I came face-to-face with God's truths about my innermost being.

Do you want to know the hardest part of my mirror fast? The hardest part was taking the papers down. You can't spend forty days with God's truth staring you in the face and *not* be changed.

My favorite part of that experiment was the fact that I didn't do it alone. My youngest daughter, Anna, covered her mirrors too. Like me, she wanted to see herself through the eyes of her Creator, who declares her beloved and beautiful.

Maria is asking us to take our daughters by the hand and invite them into a meaningful journey. You don't have to cover your mirrors. (But you may!) Here's what I can promise you: you will be guided, step-by-step, toward a realistic plan to model confidence for your daughters.

Will it be hard? Maybe. Will it ask something of us? Definitely. But I'm all in. So is Maria.

How about you and your daughters? Are you in?

Join us. Let's follow where Jesus leads.

Jennifer Dukes Lee, mom to two teenagers
and author of *It's All Under Control*,
The Happiness Dare, and *Love Idol*

Showing Her Confident

I'll never forget the first time I saw what a confident woman looked like.

I was sitting at a table at a fancy restaurant. My best friend was about to graduate from college, and we were out celebrating with a large group of her closest family and friends. At dinner, I sat next to her brother and her mom.

I can picture this moment like it was yesterday: the son, in his early twenties, sitting next to his mom and gently, one flick at a time, jiggling the skin under her arm.

You know the body part I am talking about, right? The jiggly part of our arms right under our biceps. The arm spot we try to hide in pictures. Yes, that spot. Her arm was stretched out and lying on the back of the chair next to her, and flick by flick, out of sheer boredom, he was making her arm wiggle and flap in the wind in front of an *entire* table of people. She let him. She didn't pay him any attention. It didn't bother her at *all*.

My insecure brain exploded. *Isn't that embarrassing? Won't people look at her and think she has fat on her arms? Does she even notice he is doing that? Doesn't she care what people think? Doesn't she know most women avoid arm jiggles?*

This came from the girl who has slipped in and out of pools at a careful angle her entire life to make sure *no one* ever got a clear view of her bottom. I could *not* understand *not* caring about jiggling arms. I had to learn more about this woman. I wanted to learn her secret.

As I got to know my friend's mom better, I was not disappointed. She was a woman wholly confident in who she was and completely comfortable in her own skin. It was like seeing a baby squirrel. You know they must exist, but you have never actually seen one. And guess what she instilled in her daughter? You got it—confidence.

So it's true, I thought. *Being confident and secure is possible.* And you know what? It looked good on them too. I loved eating with them, the sheer joy of enjoying yummy God-created food. I kid you not, I had to explain to my friend what calorie counting was.

Even working out with them was fun. Her mom clapped loudly while she walked or ran because she said it improved blood flow through the arms. Well, okay then. In fact, clapping did make things more fun. I saw joy and the freedom that confidence produced in them, and I wanted it. I craved it, and had to have it for myself. And I had to have it for my daughter.

The question was, How could I get there? How could I become *that* woman, and would it help my daughter? I honestly never really tried to become confident, because I didn't believe it was possible. Why bother making an effort for something I thought I could never possess? So I wrote myself off as someone who was always going to be insecure and went on my merry, messy way.

But insecurity is destructive. It doesn't stay with numbers on the scale or clothes that are too small. It seeps into friendships, careers, marriages, and definitely parenting. I thought it was all behind me because I was finally married, but the damage had only just begun. The formula is not promising: an insecure mother + crossed fingers = a daughter who will somehow magically avoid the insecurity maelstrom.

I decided to do the one thing I felt I *could* do: teach myself to be confident so that I could turn around and teach her too. After all, how could I possibly expect her to love her body, her face, her hair, her life, her uniqueness, her gifts, her everything if I didn't learn to love mine first?

Helping Our Daughters by Becoming Confident Women

I was thirteen, and I ripped them clean off my body.

I swore that those jeans had fit just the week before, and yet when I put them on that day they felt *so* tight. Too tight. As if I had gained fifty pounds and now was larger than I had ever been before, and people would make fun of my butt even more. That kind of tight.

It's crazy the toll that emotions can have on our psyche, our spiritual health, and even our physical abilities. The sadness that welled up in me was so big and powerful that I turned into a pre-teen girl Hulk who was able to tear down the seam of a sturdy pair of jeans with her own two hands.

There I sat, sobbing in a puddle of ripped material, and why? Because for that one single moment I *felt* too big.

My mom didn't know what to do with me. I didn't know what to do with me, and so we sat. We offered each other no sense of assurance that this wouldn't happen again, nor did we have any idea how to help each other. Mom understood. We both thought we had "thunder thighs" and that life would always be like this for us: the up-and-down roller coaster of thigh crunches, disordered eating, and dressing up to *try* to feel beautiful.

When I look back, I feel so sad for us. We had no hope. We had no tools to deal with our insecurity, and we just did what we could to survive the many self-demeaning lies of insecurity and poor body image.

The first day I held my daughter, this very story flashed before my eyes. New tears rolled down my cheeks as I thought, *I don't want this for her. There has got to be a way out.* I became determined to do anything and everything, even down to sacrificing my own life, if it meant equipping her with the confidence and the tools she would need to live through her own adolescent journey armed and ready.

So I did what every desperate mom does: I got on my hands and knees and prayed for God's help. I didn't know how to be confident. I didn't know what godly confidence looked like or how it differed from pride. I didn't know if it was possible to defeat the mirror or the numbers on the scale. But if God could raise a man from the dead, surely he could do this, right?

Right! I am here to tell you he can, and he did. Over the years, through the power of God's Word and his provision, I have retrained my mind to see myself and my body through new eyes and have jumped off the insecurity train. This is miraculous news! It means that if there is hope for me, there is hope for my girl. And if there is hope for my girl, there is hope for yours too.

The journey might not be smooth, and the Lord knows that at the end of the day, we are all still women. But God's power and promises trump all of that. Are we willing to fight for what we know is better? Are we willing to change our perspectives in our lives and homes and stand up against the cultural subliminal message that physical beauty is the only truth there is? Showing our daughters our confidence will be worth all the battles. We can do it, and we can do it together.

Our Confidence

We are the confidence standards in our homes. We set the tone and the example of what confidence looks like. Whether we like it or admit it, our daughters notice everything we do, and we are their best hope for confidence. They see our comings and goings, they notice the way we look at ourselves in the mirror, and they hear us mutter under our breath. The battle is on. We are in the spotlight, and we have a job to do.

It doesn't sound like much fun, does it? I know. I feel this pain right along with you. But remember, it is not a call to perfection; it is a call to *humble confidence*. It's a call to go *with* our daughters, hand in hand, toward God-filled, confident living.

First of all, we need to take up this confidence like it is ours to keep, holding it white knuckled in our hands through Christ in us. We don't have to be confident in ourselves; we need only be confident of him in us. The fact is we are already confident because God is confident. We simply need to start acting like it.

Throughout the pages of this book, we are going to look honestly and boldly at our words, choices, and actions. We are going to analyze every choice we make when it comes to our bodies and our looks, and we are going to check our motives. For the sake of our daughters, we are going to take up this cause and see what we find. Then we will show them and tell them all we have learned. The confident part? It can start today by us simply saying we *can* do this.

Want to know a secret? Want to know why I was insecure? Why we all are?

I was insecure because I thought about myself way too much. Me, myself, and I were the focus almost 24/7; I was obsessed with me. Doesn't it make sense? Our minds protest that surely we are doing nothing wrong. We are simply trying to improve ourselves, become better. So we size ourselves up on a minute-to-minute basis and live in denial of the fact that doing so is wrong. The truth is I never had the strength to be any different because I didn't have the motivation to change.

Then I met Jesus. He held up a mirror to my life and revealed something that stopped me dead in my tracks. His presence and his words seared deep into my soul: *Maria, you want to become confident? You want to live free from obsessing over your body? Take your eyes off of you and fix them on me instead.*

Forget the mirror altogether. Then confidence can be ours. Paul tells us, "Such confidence we have through Christ before God.

Not that we are competent in ourselves to claim anything for ourselves, but our competence comes from God" (2 Cor. 3:4–5). He also says:

> So, I find this law at work: Although I want to do good, evil is right there with me. For in my inner being I delight in God's law; but I see another law at work in me, waging war against the law of my mind and making me a prisoner of the law of sin at work within me. What a wretched man I am! Who will rescue me from this body that is subject to death? Thanks be to God, who delivers me through Jesus Christ our Lord! (Rom. 7:21–25)

I *am* wretched! I was right all along. I kept staring at myself in the mirror, waiting and hoping something would change. If I tried hard enough, maybe I could actually be better. But every workout class, every bite of food, every insecurity-based decision and self-demeaning word were based on the faulty idea that human perfection can be found, that eventually I could find a way to fix me. The truth is *we* can't fix ourselves. In fact, that is why Jesus had to come. All our chasing, all our wandering, all our insecurities are leading our girls into the wilderness when we seek to find a *goodness* in us that does not exist apart from God.

In actuality, our bodies are not perfect. And no, all our decisions are not always the right ones. Yes, we do say things that hurt people, and we *will* have failures. That is why we need Jesus. The perfection we seek will not come until the day we see him face-to-face. Because God is good, it is in our weaknesses that God makes us confident and strong.

I don't want to chase after the wind anymore. I know you don't want your daughter to chase after the wind either. Will you stop with me? Together, let's commit to making the choice today to be confident—not in ourselves, or in anything we can or cannot do, but in the God who lives in us.

Security is in us. It always has been. When we think insecure thoughts or act on our lack of self-confidence, we make the decision to hand our security away. It is ours to control, not the other way around.

We can't fake it anymore. Our daughters are keen and smart, and they will see right through our acts. If we want to show them what a confident woman looks like, we have to *be* confident. If we want our girls to know that beauty comes from within and that the size of our jeans doesn't measure our worth, we have to believe it for ourselves too.

The Importance of Confidence

Our daughters are being sought after and sold a bag of lies. It is *loud* out there, and if they do not have the confidence to stick to what they believe to be good and true, the risks do not end at insecurity. We are not talking about becoming confident for its own sake. Confidence in *who we are as God's beautiful creations* protects us from harming ourselves and others.

Insecurity Can Lead to an Eating Disorder

Eating is an easy first fix. I was in seventh grade when I skipped my first meal, and it felt good to be in control. Many girls turn to anorexia or bulimia because nothing else has worked to get rid of the hatred they have for themselves and the way they look. When you control what you eat, you can trick yourself into believing you are heading toward a happier place where you don't hate the way you look.

Insecurity Can Lead to Promiscuity

Getting attention from boys is a surefire way to temporarily forget your insecurities. Unfortunately, most teens do not have the self-control not to cross the line once they are faced with it. Too many girls give themselves over to physical intimacy because their need for attention has led them down a road they cannot turn back from. Perhaps it's the first time a boy has looked their way. Perhaps they've learned how to make sure, with actions and attire, that attention always comes their way. Whether it's out of the fear of being rejected or being made fun of, girls continue to give in and regularly participate in physical relationships. They may think, *Once I lose my virginity, what is the point of trying to stay pure?* Young girls are trading in their bodies at ever-increasing rates and at ever-decreasing ages. In their article "Teens: Oral Sex and Casual Prostitution No Biggie," Claire Shipman and Cole Kazdin, writers for *Good Morning America*, comment:

> After four years researching for the documentary, Azam told "Good Morning America" that oral sex is as common as kissing for teens and that casual prostitution—being paid at parties to strip, give sexual favors or have sex—is far more commonplace than once believed.[1]

Insecurity Can Lead to Self-Harm

Cutting was something new to me. The first time one of the girls in our junior high youth group told me she had been struggling with cutting, I had no idea what it even was. Cutting was not popular or prominent in my generation, but today teens experiment with it just to see what it feels like. One of our leaders had struggled with cutting and, thankfully, was able to help and guide many of our youth through healing and recovery. When she gave her testimony at youth group one night, she shared, "I was numb on the inside, and I wanted to make sure I was still able to feel. Cutting was my way of reminding myself that I was still alive." Cutting, like eating disorders, is a form of control. When everyone else seems to be telling them what to do and nothing seems to be going right, cutting is a way for teens to take back what they feel they have lost. A common thought is, *If I cannot control what is going on in my life, at least I can control this.* And not only that, but physical pain is a way for them to forget about the emotional pain they are feeling. Emotional pain is hard to deal with, so when physical pain helps them to forget, they become addicted to forgetting. The Mayo Clinic does a good job of not only explaining cutting but also linking the majority of self-harm to teenagers.

> Self-injury is the act of deliberately harming the surface of your own body, such as cutting or burning yourself. It's typically not meant as a suicide attempt. Rather, this type of self-injury is an unhealthy way to cope with emotional pain, intense anger, and frustration. . . .
> Most people who self-injure are teenagers. . . . Self-injury often starts in the early teen years, when emotions are more volatile and teens face increasing peer pressure, loneliness, and conflicts with parents or other authority figures.[2]

This explanation is not meant to scare us but to remind us of the importance of what we are setting out to do. Society has tried. It has redefined beauty with clothing ads that now glorify curves and differences. *Beauty* no longer necessarily means skinny, and there are organizations aimed at reminding us that beauty comes from within. But it's not enough. Our daughters are ours to influence first and foremost. May we take them up under our own confident wing, may we model for them what humble confidence looks like, and may our lives be a constant reminder of the importance of godly confidence.

Confident Mom
CHALLENGE

Challenge #1: Let's make a commitment. Let's put pen to paper and promise to try. Our journey toward godly confidence might not always look pretty, and at times we might be tempted to become discouraged, but I believe we can do it. We must do it. Use the commitment that follows or feel free to write your own, but take a moment now to truly commit to the challenges laid out for you in these pages.

I, _____, make a commitment to learn more about what my daughter is going through as a young woman in the world today and to do everything I can to be there for her in a supportive and loving way. I know that I might not be able to understand all she is going through, that I am going to make mistakes along the way, and that sometimes it is going to be very hard, but I commit to making a conscious effort as her parent to have an intentional impact on her life. I will change some of my own behaviors to make my home a place where confidence grows.

_____

Mom's Signature

_____

Date

Confident Daughter
DISCUSSION QUESTIONS

In this section in each chapter, you will find questions to discuss with your girl. You can even confess to her that you are reading this book and tell her "the book is making me do it!" These questions are not for the purpose of pulling information out of your daughter but for intermingling your heart with hers. You can put these questions in your back pocket for an impromptu kitchen chat or print them out and take them with you on a coffee date. You can pray over them first and then share them with your girl when you are ready, or you can use them in a small group setting. However you use them is up to you, but may they prompt you toward honesty, healing, and confidence every step of the way.

1. Have you ever seen a confident woman? What was she like? What did you admire about her?
2. Do you consider yourself to be a confident person? Why or why not?

3. Read 2 Corinthians 3:4–5 and Romans 7:21–25. What truths about confidence in God's Word hit you the hardest? Why?

4. What are the top two things you desire most for your life?

5. What is an example of a self-demeaning thought you struggle with? Do you believe it is possible to defeat those thoughts for good?

6. God wants you to be free and have God-centered confidence. Do you believe this is possible? Why or why not? Are you willing to try together?

7. What are some of your greatest hesitations or fears in fighting for confidence in your life?

8. If you feel comfortable, share your goals and your fears and lift them up in prayer.

A Mom's Prayer

God, we confess to you that we don't feel confident, but we are coming to you because we want to be. We want to take up your truth and remember that confidence is ours through you and you alone. Would you help us to remember? When we are feeling down, when we are feeling less than, would you help us to remember the importance of our God-given confidence? We know that our girls need us to be confident for them, and so we pray for the strength to become the best example of a confident, godly woman that they have ever seen. Father, you are a God of miracles, and we are praying for the miracle of confidence for our families and in our homes. Amen.

two

Naming Your Story

*D*id you love yourself growing up?

When you look back, do you think on your youth fondly? Do you see confidence? Do you see worth? Do you see security?

I pray that you do. I pray that you were one of the few who dodged waking up in the morning and feeling like you had holes in your heart to fill. I pray that you grew up confident, secure, and loving your body just as it was. I pray that was you.

If that wasn't you, then I wonder if you grew up the way I did: always feeling like there was something wrong with me, always trying to fix something about myself but with no idea how to. I did anything and everything to fill the gaps in my self-worth, often hurting myself in the process. You name it—eating disorders, boys, pills, parties, perfectionism—I tried it all. All of it failed me.

We cannot take away all the hurt for our daughters, but we can hurt alongside them. We can help them carry their burdens—and any hurt that life may bring. For as long as they are ours to hold, we can fight for them and with them. Soon they will be gone; they will be up and moved and out of our homes. But for now they are ours, and they need moms who are strong enough to name their own stories.

Our Stories

I am writing to you as a daughter who wished she had known how to ask her parents for help. My parents were always there for me and would have done anything for me, but a nine-year-old girl does not know how to make sense of what is going on inside her nor how to communicate it clearly. But I remember it all like it was yesterday, and I can communicate it *now*.

As a young girl with growing hips and plummeting self-worth, the struggle and the torment my young mind experienced wreaked havoc on my choices. My deepest prayer is that our own stories might help us better see the world through our daughters' eyes. I am writing this book because I believe passionately that there is hope for our daughters, even in the midst of the madness in which they are growing up.

Parents, believe it or not, you have the ability and the influence, with God as your strength, to help protect your daughters from the very things that destroy the way they look at themselves. Together may we guide them to the very God who gives life and restoration to the areas we need it most.

What is your story? Our stories are part of us whether we cover them up or not.

Every week my husband and I look forward to date night. We put a movie on for the kids inside, and we dine on some takeout together outside. Many date nights we spend just catching up or sharing how our day was. Other nights we do silly things such as make a list of our top ten favorite movies of all time. Then there are those nights when something gets stirred up. From the depths of the muck and mire one night, my husband asked me this question: "So, how many boyfriends did you have before me?"

Um, I'm sorry, what?!

I thought we were past this. Fourteen years and five kids later, I thought that surely the ghosts of my past would no longer be brought up. I am whole, I am made new in Jesus, and I don't even mind my curves anymore. Why this? Why now?

I sat there silently staring at him, praying that a comet would shoot down from the sky and take me to be with Jesus now! Maybe if I stared at him long enough, he would forget that he asked.

"Well," he said, "just tell me. It's no big deal, but I just realized I don't know that part of your story."

Duh! You don't know that part of my story because I prefer it didn't exist. It hurt; two decades later it still hurts. What followed was a tearful explanation of my youth, one I had thought I could leave behind me, yet here it was again.

But you know what? Though digging it up *was* heart wrenching, it was also healing. Hearing my husband give me sweet words of love and adoration despite my choices gave me a glimpse of how God sees me. This level of grace is a gift we can also give to our daughters.

Would we allow them the honor of hearing some of the painful parts of our stories? Would we allow them the privilege and trust of seeing our tears and our most vulnerable places?

There is no doubt that our stories are impacting our daughters. We may not mean to, but we are all carrying our stuff and passing it down. However, it doesn't need to be a negative thing. Instead of unintentionally dumping our junk on them, we can intentionally dig through the pieces, identify the places we need healing, and hand to our daughters our newfound hope. With a smile on our faces and joy in our hearts, may we hand them our redemptive stories.

Finding Redemption

First, let's leave our shame at the door.

Walk to the front door wherever you are, open it, lift off your shoulders the invisible and heavy load of shame you carry, put it down, close the door, and walk away. Shame makes us hide; shame makes us bend truths and keep secrets. Shame makes us run away from Jesus when what he wants is for us to run *to him*. Trust me, I know the feeling. Friends, none of us skip the shame, and for the sake of proving to you that you are not alone, I will share one of my most shame-inducing moments: in college, I was arrested. Arrested. (Please, Lord Jesus, let my children not read this book until they are at least forty-two. Thank you. Amen.) Talk about shame carrying. I was walking home from a party my freshman year. I did not yet know Jesus or the confidence he offers us, and drinking was just what you did on the weekends. The police in my college town prided themselves on picking up students who had been drinking to teach them a lesson. It was a lesson I learned well. I spent a night in jail, concrete floor and all.

It's amazing to think back on how God was working in my life even before I knew him. In the years before I confessed Jesus as Lord, he was walking with me, watching me, and tracking each and every step of my journey. When I went to court, there was a gracious and merciful substitute judge. I stood there and sobbed to him my story. Wow, did I sob. All the shame and embarrassment of this perfectionist came pouring out before him. He dropped the charges. He dropped all the charges: no conviction, no record, no guilt. Free from everything except for the shame.

To this day, every time I fill out an application my heart stops at the question, "Have you ever been convicted of a crime?" (Gulp.) Well, no, but I should have been.

Talk about unworthy to do anything, *especially* serve God. No, not me, I wasn't good enough. Parts of my story feel so ugly and dark. But I believe God wants to use our stories for freedom and for his glory.

This incident in college was the very thing that began to bring my heart to Jesus. My dad picked up his jailbird daughter, sat across the table from me, and shared his testimony. "Maria," he said, "it is like I found a gift in my relationship with Jesus, and it is a gift I so badly want to share with you." And then Jesus whispered in my heart, "You find shame in the very things that remind you how much you need me."

Jesus is not ashamed of our stories, so why should we be? "Here is a trustworthy saying that deserves full acceptance: Christ Jesus came into the world to save sinners—of whom I am the worst" (1 Tim. 1:15). This is the beauty of the cross and the beauty of the hope we have to offer to our daughters. Jesus did not come because we are perfect; he came because we are not! He doesn't expect us to be perfect. We need to shout this to the heights so that our daughters will hear us. We need to cut the perfect-parent act. Our children will learn far more from our mistakes and our honesty than they will from our "I have it all together."

Growing up, I remember feeling so alone. I couldn't really trust my friends, I didn't want to disappoint the adults in my life, and I didn't know how to cope with all the confusing feelings I was experiencing. I needed an honest voice, one that would reach out to me and say, "You are going to be okay. Do you know how I know? Because I am okay. May I tell you my story?"

We are going to take plenty of time in this book to dig through the *how-tos* of modeling confidence. But for now, let's pause at the *whys*. Take this opportunity to allow your brain to venture back to the days when you were young. How did you feel? What was it like? What hurt you most? What mistakes did you make? If you are feeling brave, write it down as a story, tell it to a friend, or practice it on your husband. Ready your heart and mind now for sharing with your daughter later.

As I write, my daughter is eleven. No, she does not yet know that Mommy went to jail or that I took diet pills to cope with my insecurity. She is too young for those parts of my story. But I am ready to share those things when it is the right time. Whether your daughter is one or nineteen, going through this process now will prepare you for whenever the time comes. I have prayed through all the bits and pieces of my story, and I keep them in my back pocket. I continually pray for God's wisdom and discernment as to *when to share*. But it is no longer a question of if, it's when.

I think a good rule of thumb as to when to share is to match your age at the time of your story to the current age of your daughter. If your daughter is seven, twelve, or fifteen, think back to how you felt at her age. Are there any shareable experiences?

This past year, my daughter was invited to her first sleepover party. My husband and I talked about it, and we had to go with our gut—we just weren't ready to allow her to go. I lay with her in bed, and my very disappointed daughter did not fully understand the no she had just received. It was time for me to share.

"Honey," I said, "when I was exactly your age, I was invited to my first sleepover party. I was in third grade, and there were about six of us girls there. We were up all night, and we talked about things and did things that my parents had taught me were not good. To this day, I still remember what we talked about, and, honey, I don't want you to experience those things yet. I don't think you want to experience them either. I know you don't understand, but God gave you to me to love and protect you, and I am asking you to just trust me on this one."

That was enough for her. She might not have liked that she could not go, but she trusted my judgment because I had been there.

You have been places too. All of your places were strategically allowed by your heavenly Father for such a time as this.

Parent Wounds and Prayer

For better or for worse, we are parents now, and we toggle constantly between praying that we never end up like our parents and realizing that we are becoming just like them. It's okay to live in both of those places, but let's capitalize on them. May we identify the pieces of our youth that we want to bring with us into our own parenting and may we leave behind the things we don't.

My parents were awesome at the big things. When life hit the fan, they never made me feel bad or condemned. It was in the smaller, everyday moments that I felt less than and not good enough. As an adult, God has used my passion and bridled it for his good. But as a youth, my emotions and passions ran amok. I mouthed off constantly and never thought I was wrong.

I've heard it said that raising a teen girl is like taming a wild horse, and the key is not to make her feel bad for her wildness as she grows into maturity. In my own parenting, I try to remember daily that we are in the training years.

Good: staying calm in disaster.

Bad: making my daughter feel shame for not being tame yet.

As we head into this journey together, I want you to know I am with you. We are not perfect parents, nor will we ever be. But I have seen God's work in me as he tamed me from a crazy, wild horse into his confident steed.

God wants to heal the wounds you carry from your teenage years and wants you to learn from them so that you can better help your daughter wade through her own adolescent and teen years. Take some time to pray for yourself and your daughter. Pray for God to use your youth to make you a better parent. Don't underestimate the worth of the road God used to bring you to where you are now.

CHALLENGE

The Confident Mom Challenge sections in the remaining chapters are where you throw caution to the wind and just give them a try! Some challenges are tougher than others, and some you might flat out not want to do. I pray though that you will give them a go. I pray that you will go out on a limb and just try—no matter how crazy it sounds!

Bring your daughter along with you! Share the challenge with her at her level of maturity. This is a confident mom *and* confident daughter journey. It is going to be risky, but I've been praying for God to pay back big dividends for your courage.

Challenge #2: In this chapter, let's start off with boldness—share your story. No matter the age of your daughter, sit her down and share an age-appropriate story about your youth.

Bonus Challenge: Find a trusted friend and tell them your *whole* story, including all the nitty-gritty and embarrassing pieces.

Confident Daughter
DISCUSSION QUESTIONS

1. Moms, think back to your teen years, and, daughters, think back three years ago. What was that age like for you? What feelings do you get when you think about those times?

2. What are your top three good memories from that age? What are your top three bad memories from that age?

3. What are some things you learned from those years that God used in your life?

4. Moms, what are a few things that you experienced when you were your daughter's age that you are praying will be different for her?

5. Moms, are there some things your parents did that you hated?

6. Daughters, what are some things that your parents do now that you don't like?

7. Moms, what are some things that your parents did that you loved and/or appreciated?

8. Daughters, what are some things that your parents do that you love and/or appreciate?

9. What are some stories from your lives that you can share to give each other a better understanding of who you are and why you are the way you are today?

10. Read 1 Timothy 1:15. What stands out to you about this verse?

A Mom's Prayer

Father, you know our stories. You knew each day of our lives before one of them came to be, and we take hope in knowing that you can use our pain for your purposes. We ask you, Lord, to redeem our stories. Will you give us the words we need to identify our past hurts and pains, and would you help us discern when it is time to share with our girls? We would lay down our lives for our daughters; we would do anything for them! Help us to have the strength to do whatever is necessary. We thank you for our own parents. For better or worse, may you help us learn from their examples. Thank you for being with us now, Lord. This journey is hard; may it be fruitful according to your will. In the powerful and redeeming name of Jesus we pray. Amen.

three

If We Don't, Then Who Will?

The sad truth is I would not be writing this book if this were only about having a poor self-image. Sure, it is no fun to look in the mirror and hate what you see, but the problem for young women is that their self-image issue doesn't end there. The mirror is simply where it starts. The pain of this struggle seeps into the cracks of their very beings. Because most girls are so young when the struggle begins, they do not know how to cope with disappointing and self-destructive thoughts. As a result, their poor self-image affects their actions, words, thoughts, behaviors, and decisions. It is, in fact, a dark cloud that looms over their lives every minute of every day. I know because I lived it.

Every time I looked in the mirror, I paid close attention to every detail of my body. What was too big, what was too small, what wasn't perfect—it consumed my thoughts. The pain followed me everywhere, and it began to feel unbearable.

It hurt to look in the mirror and hate what I saw. It hurt that though deep down inside I knew there was nothing wrong with me, I was unable to believe it. It hurt to go through each day, looking intently at other girls and keeping track of what they were wearing and how they looked and comparing myself to them. It was most hurtful to feel like I had no control over any of these negative thoughts. My preteen shoulders could not handle the pain, and I needed to start *doing* something to try to stop it.

I convinced myself very early on that I was not doing anything wrong. What if I didn't want to eat lunch? I simply wasn't hungry. Every day, I set my lunch in front of me for a little while, and then when everyone else was about done, I walked over to the trash can and threw it all away. At dinner, I ate just enough to make it look like I was eating, but I never cleaned my plate. All of this made me feel a little better, as if I was finally in control. But as I grew older and more mature, so did my coping mechanisms, and the obsession with boys began.

It was the typical teenage scene: my two best friends and I liked the same guy. Each of us had equally low views of ourselves, so you can imagine the lengths we were willing to go to get his attention. My choices about what to wear, how to act, and how far I would go physically with a boy were based solely on my desire to feel good about who I was. In hindsight, to an eighth-grade girl, attention from a boy is like a drug. It gives you a temporary sense that you are on top of the world. For those moments, you feel good about yourself, you feel wanted, you feel beautiful. But like every drug, the risks are far greater than the rewards. When I came down off the high of getting unhealthy attention, I went home and cried, knowing I had said and done things I would never be able to undo.

As I got older, the game I was playing got tougher, and it became easy to get my hands on other things to help me in my trek to "freedom." Diet pills became a regular part of my life, as did partying and drinking with friends. As I look back on those days, I cannot emphasize enough how painful they were. I was fighting with all my might to find something that did not exist, and all along the way, I compromised who I was as a woman. Ecclesiastes 2:11 puts it perfectly: "Yet when I surveyed all that my hands had done and what I had toiled to achieve, everything was meaningless, a chasing after the wind; nothing was gained under the sun." Nothing at all was gained, but many, many things were lost.

The saddest part was that deep down, I knew I did not want my life to be that way. I just did not have the strength, self-confidence, or self-worth to stand up to the world I was living in, a world that told me, around every corner, having sex fulfills, dressing provocatively makes you beautiful, and partying is the best way to have fun. I was not important enough to myself to make tough choices, and I was too ashamed to ask for help.

I praise God every day that he did not give up on me, even when I already had. One day in my sophomore year in college, I had taken one too many diet pills and found myself curled up in bed, unable to move. That was it. I was at rock bottom. The following years of my life were marked by a new journey: the journey to discover who God was and his plan for my life. What helped me the most was being able to take my eyes off myself for the very first time and focus my time and energy on something greater. Finally, at the age of twenty, I found the perspective and hope I had been looking for all along. I found Christ.

Throughout this book, I will share exactly what God did in my life, but for now, I want to go back to your daughter. I have been praying for your daughter for years, praying that God would protect her from all that I lived through at such a young age. I believe that she does not have to live like that, and if my years of being in that terrible place can help you bring her refuge, then I thank God that he allowed me to live through it.

Please take some time as you read through this book to pay attention to the world your daughter is living in. She is crying out for your help but is scared to ask. She wants to be strong but does not have the strength.

I know that, right now, you might feel like the world is on your shoulders, and I do not mean to scare or burden you. But our daughters are facing a huge battle for their hearts, and not nearly enough people are trying to help them fight it. The culture that your daughter is growing up in influences her 24/7 to think a certain way, act a certain way, and look a certain way. It is time for you to fight back 24/7. Your daughter's life depends on it.

What about my parents? Did they notice? What did they do? I am sure that my parents knew a little bit about my insecurities. But I think insecurity was expected then: women don't like their bodies, that's just the way it is, they all feel that way. I appeared happy on the outside. I was good at sports, playing volleyball and softball. I did great in school, always bringing home good grades and excelling in college-level courses. I was a good kid who worked hard and appeared to love life. But my parents, peers, teachers, and coaches had no idea of the extent that I was willing to go to feel better about myself and to fix the mind battle in which I lived. I was excellent at hiding.

If our girls are great at hiding, then what do we parents have to do? We have to get even better at knowing. We must begin to pray for God to show us what is there instead of seeing only what we want to see. It's our job. It is not an easy one, not a job for the faint of heart. But if we don't do it, who will?

Not *My* Daughter!

You might be thinking right now, *Not my daughter!* Not my daughter either. Let's just agree to close the book and live in blissful ignorance. I'd much rather live on that island of thought than the one that allows my mom brain to picture my daughter in pain. Ugh, I don't want to go there either. But I'll go if you will.

It is tempting to look at a daughter who you believe is beautiful, confident, and wonderful and assume she could not possibly be going through a struggle with self-image. I understand. I step into my daughter's room. I size up her sleeping body from head to toe, and I am in awe of her. She is everything. She is perfect. She is mine. She is innocent.

And she is human.

I've lived long enough to realize she is going to experience hurt. There will be pain in her life, and it is my job as a mom to be ready. If I am not ready, then who will be?

Through years of working with junior high students and parents, I know that the worst thing to plague a parent's ability to help his or her child is the inability to see past what they want to see. You want to think that your daughter has it all together and that the way she acts inside your home is exactly how she acts when in school, on social media, and out with friends. We see our daughters and we see the babies they started as. But there we stand alone. The world is treating our girls as if they are older. Even if your daughter wants to stay young and innocent (which many girls have the sincere desire to do), she is not equipped with the right tools to stand up on her own to the pressures on her. Let me paint you a picture.

For most children, the home is a safe place, a place where they can play and be themselves and not worry about people's expectations or what others think of them. It is, for the most part, quiet and free from pressure. (Ideally, by the end of this book, you will know how to make your home completely safe and free of pressure.) Now picture your daughter walking out of that quiet place into one that fills her life and head with noise: *In order to get Ben to like you, you need to give him what he wants. The new style is short shorts. If you don't wear them, you won't get any attention. All of your friends are going to a movie on Friday, but you know your parents won't let you go. What are you going to do? Ava found out you were talking about her, and now she is turning all your friends against you. There is a party Saturday night. You had fun last time you drank, so you should go. That guy in science class keeps flirting with you, saying sexual things to you. You don't have to act on it but go along with it. It's fun. Instagram is full of girls posing in skimpy clothes. There's no harm in it. It's just a picture. You know that is what people want to see.*

I wish I were exaggerating.

If your daughter is younger, I pray she is not yet in this world. But kids start dating in kindergarten now, and third graders have phones. It is not too soon to be ready. We must prepare.

I will be the first one to admit that not all girls struggle with these issues on the same scale. I have had many friends throughout my life who were bothered with them much less often and less severely than I was growing up. Thankfully, I believe there are some telltale signs of what might be going on behind the closed doors of your daughter's mind. I am going to give you a list that might help, but before I do, I would like to share a gentle insight.

As we read through this list together, I pray that our hearts stay steady and calm. If our daughters do some of these things, it's okay. We have not failed as parents, and there is still plenty of time to turn this ship around. We are simply taking a step back to observe and ask why. Many of these behaviors are typical *teenageness*; however, let's take the opportunity in this book to dig below the surface.

If your daughter is younger, log these signs away in the back of your mind. I have to be honest with you; when I wrote the first version of this book, my daughter was two. Now, eight years later, when I reread the list, I about had a heart attack. I had kept the blinders on. I had allowed myself to get stuck in the illusion that my little girl was going to stay little forever. It's time for the scales to come off and the radar to go up. My aching mommy heart said a quick prayer: *Jesus, I am going to need your help constantly with this. Will you please come with me? I can't do this alone.*

He's got us. Let's go.

Signs Your Daughter Is Struggling (or Thinking about It)

She Spends Most of Her Time at Home in Seclusion

By seclusion, I mean locked away in her room or glued to the computer, where you really have no idea what she is doing. If she does not want you to see or know what she is doing, trust me, there is a reason. Not that it is automatically a bad reason, but a regular pop in with a "How are you doing, honey?" might be a great help to remind her not only that you are there but also how much you care.

Anything She Does on the Computer Is Top Secret

You could not find her Facebook page, Instagram account, text messages, or Snapchats even if you wanted to. She is diligent about making sure you cannot find what she is doing while she is on the internet. There is no good reason for her online interactions to not stand up to the light of day.

She Sometimes (or Oftentimes) Makes Comments about Her Body, Good or Bad

Even if it is in a joking manner, making comments about the way she looks is a sign that your daughter is looking for affirmation in a place where she is hurting. I remember constantly making such comments to my parents in the hope that one magical time when they told me "You are beautiful" or "You are perfect," it would change the way I thought about myself. Your daughter's words about herself just might be a cry for help from you.

She Is Very Aware of What She Eats

This can look like a wide variety of things, anything from looking like she merely has a concern for eating healthy to being obsessed with not eating carbohydrates, sweets, or fatty foods. Of course, there is nothing wrong with eating healthy, but when a twelve-year-old is pointedly asking for carrot sticks instead of cookies in her lunch, there is likely a reason for it. Or when your nine-year-old daughter who used to beg for ice cream sundaes on the weekends doesn't anymore, it may be more than just simply growing up.

Boys, Boys, Boys (Gag), and More Boys

I have been around hundreds and hundreds of girls throughout my life, whether as an adolescent or a leader in youth group. Believe me, the ones who are most obsessed with boys are the ones who struggle the most with their self-image. The confident girls, the ones who have somehow eluded this insecurity plague, care much less about boys or what they think. Why? Because they can take them or leave them; they don't *need* boys in order to feel good about themselves. Thus, the formula goes like this: the healthier the view of self = the healthier the view of boys.

She Is Always Wearing Revealing Clothing

It seems counterintuitive that a girl who struggles with the way she looks would want to show off as much of her body as she can, but the important question to ask yourself is, *What does my daughter look like when she walks out the door?* Moms especially like to think that their daughters just look cute or pretty, but ask yourself objectively, *Is more of my daughter's skin showing than is covered? Does her outfit reveal every curve?* Let's agree right here and now to have a realistic view of the clothes our daughters wear.

She Is Very Knowledgeable of All That Goes On in Hollywood

There is something about Hollywood celebs that just sucks us in. They are way prettier and cooler than we are, their social media feeds are amazing, and, therefore, they must be way more trustworthy, right? Wrong. But unfortunately, it might seem that way to our daughters. Hollywood does an excellent job of painting a certain picture about life, one that is entirely unrealistic and unhealthy. The more engulfed your daughter is in that world, the less involved she is in what is real and healthy.

You Are the Enemy

To teenagers, we may be way uncool, but we should not be the enemy. However, there are many reasons why our daughters might consider us to be the enemy. They might think we are trying to rain on their parade, or they might be paranoid that if we find out certain things about them, we will be angry or disappointed. No matter the reason, they will try to keep you at arm's length.

I believe there is always hope for our relationships with our daughters. The key is for us to see hope and see the need for change. My prayer is that this list will be a tool to help us zero in on certain behavioral patterns that our daughters might have or might develop. If my parents had had this list when I was young, they would have checked off every one of them. We need to be set up for success, and our first step is honest awareness. Step two? Get ready for battle.

It's Time to Fight

It is our job to offer our children the wisdom of God. "My son [or daughter], do not let wisdom and understanding out of your sight, preserve sound judgment and discretion; they will be life for you, an ornament to grace your neck" (Prov. 3:21–22).

It is our job to impress God's Word on our hearts and make it known in our homes.

It is our job to model for our children that God's Word is not a burden, is not a list of dos and don'ts, and is not condemning. God's Word is the hope that we cling to, and it's life for our weary bones. It's to be the accessory that we choose to put on each and every day, not because we're required to but because we need to.

There is a battle going on. Society's standards for women and teens have changed drastically from generation to generation. The world your daughter is living in is unimaginably *different* from the world we grew up in.

Walt Mueller has been a voice educating and encouraging parents since 1990 to understand and learn about the new world in which the next generation lives. He is the founder of CPYU (Center for Parent/Youth Understanding), and he writes:

> Everything's happening at younger and younger ages. This phenomenon is known as "age compression." Marketers have used it as a strategy to expand a product's market by pushing adult-type products, values and attitudes on kids at younger ages. What's resulted is an environment where what used to be for 18-year-olds is now for six-year-olds, who are increasingly dressing, talking and acting like yesterday's 18-year-olds. Some of the most direct effects can be seen in what children at younger and younger ages know and believe about sexuality, materialism, and violence. The children in your life are far less innocent and far more jaded than their peers in previous generations.[1]

A study of girls ages eleven to seventeen called *Voices of a Generation: Teenage Girls on Sex, School, and Self* by the American Association of University Women Educational Foundation had similar results:

> Regardless of age, girls who comment on the social and cultural standards of female adolescence interpret them as problematic and in some ways unrealistic or distortive roles. A few girls write specifically of mourning a childhood that at age 14, in their minds, has already evaporated. "I would like to know if 'all' girls in high school want freedom but still want to be like the little girl they were," writes a 14-year-old from Salt Lake City. An older girl from Philadelphia echoes, "I'm only 16 years old but I feel like I've been around the world twice."

Other girls explain that childhood has been replaced for them by a disorienting admixture of adulthood, sexual innocence, and sexual maturity that constitutes the social script of female adolescence.[2]

Things have changed drastically when it comes to sexual standards. When I was in high school, it was acceptable for girls to sleep with their boyfriends. Sadly, at my high school it was, in fact, what you were expected to do if you had a boyfriend. However, sleeping with many guys or with someone else's boyfriend got you a bad reputation.

In the past, people's sex lives were kept mostly private. Plastering your sexuality all over the internet was not being done yet. It was well-known that parents did not want you to have sex, and most of my peers did everything they could to hide their promiscuity from their parents. Today, things are very different. Provocative pictures and conversations about sex happen regularly online, and conversations with parents about sex consist of birth control measures. Sex is becoming part of what defines you as a woman. Culture says you need to be free to explore your sexuality in whatever way you desire. It is no longer taboo to sleep with someone you are not in a relationship with, and relationships now, more than ever, are defined by sex.

Why am I telling you all this? It is a small picture of the battlefield, a very small picture. There are entire books dedicated to revealing the situation our daughters are in. The cultural standard that makes our girls think they are less than beautiful is out there. We know it, we see it, and yet we stand crippled, not knowing what to do.

We must do something. We must be the truth tellers! We have to be the example, instead of the lady on Instagram who has eighty thousand followers for her bathing suit pics.

We are good enough.

We are important.

And if we don't stand up in our homes for our daughters, then who will?

Standing Up for Character and Letting Go of Control

I want to fix *all the things*.

I want to get my fingers in there, control the outcomes, and make sure that everything turns out great for my daughter.

I definitely want to make sure I fix her so that she doesn't have to deal with insecurity, body hatred, "big butt" name-calling in school, and boys objectifying her body. I *need* to fix that.

It's why we are going through this book together. We all want to fix things for our daughters, make life better for them, because we love them more than anything in the world.

I have some hard news. We can't fix things for them, but we can set the example for how (with God's help) they can fix things themselves.

We can take up our identity in God, model his character, and let go of control.

I have been fighting this confidence battle for young women for a decade now, and time and time again this issue of control comes up when I am talking to moms. When they realize that many of the solutions I offer in this book include letting go of control over their daughters and instead building up their own confidence, some get fidgety and uncomfortable. I often get some form of this question: "But isn't it important for me to make sure my daughter is being healthy and caring for her body?"

It is important, and I think for the first ten years of a child's life it is one of the most important things we can model for them. But we are talking about adolescence, and there are many people in our daughters' lives caring for their physical well-being. They have their PE teacher, health class, and doctors, and most schools nowadays prioritize physical health. I spent a few years as a junior varsity volleyball coach and guess what we taught our players about? Physical health.

If we combine our first decade of teaching in the home with their current physical health educators, I am positive that our daughters know that carrot sticks are good for their bodies and soda is not. We have much bigger fish to fry. We are on the battlefield for their hearts, spirits, and minds. Sisters, I pray that you might consider temporarily putting down the physical health war. Let others carry that baton for a little while, and join me instead in spending our valuable momma sweat and tears over her character and her character alone. It is a vastly important job, and I don't want one single thing taking my energy away from it.

You may think I am crazy, so I checked my theory with a pediatrician, and shortly I'll share my interview with her. But before I do, I want to take a second to talk up her and all the other amazing pediatricians out there.

God has given us a gift through medicine and through the good doctors who practice it. We don't have to constantly worry about our children's bodies, because we have someone who is watching over them for us. They give us the immense freedom to focus on the things that doctors cannot. If their doctors are not worried about their shape, size, weight, and body type, then we shouldn't worry either.

I pray that as you read these words by Dr. Kymberly Selden, they will enlighten you as much as they enlightened me. I was both educated and encouraged by Dr. Selden and the stances of the American Academy of Pediatrics that she shared with me.

I share this interview at the start of the book to get the physical health questions for our daughters addressed and to give us an idea of the type of questions we should be asking.

From an Expert on Physical Health

Dr. Selden is a local pediatrician right around the corner from where I live. She describes pediatric medicine as the perfect marriage of her love of science and children with her desire to help people. Dr. Selden forges partnerships with parents when it comes to caring for their children. She helps families create healthy lifestyles, manage minor illnesses, and recognize signs of serious illness. She and her husband have two sons and a daughter who love visual and performing arts, sports, and dance.

This is our interview.

Q: Moms are wired to protect our children, so when we have the desire to protect our daughters from a high BMI [body mass index is a calculation of our weight and height to help determine physical health], what are we protecting them from?

A: BMI has been found to be a very reliable marker for disease burdens later in life. Hypertension, diabetes, menstrual problems, polycystic ovarian syndrome, coronary artery disease, orthopedic problems, and psychosocial consequences are all examples of health issues that have been accurately linked to high BMI levels. The trend is alarming.

There is a very large range of what is considered a healthy BMI. Anywhere from 5 percent to 85 percent is considered normal, and this accounts for the fact that we all have different body types. Someone who is strong, plays sports, and lifts weights may have more muscle mass. Due to these activities, there may be no cause for concern even if their BMI is on the higher end. A person's BMI should be viewed within the context of their overall lifestyle.

We also watch for this trend over time. We don't just look at BMI in adolescence; we track it from toddlerhood so that we can see risk factors before children even get into their teen years.

Q: Say you have a young woman come into your office whose BMI is high. How do you communicate that, knowing that young women have the tendency to hear "I'm fat" even if that is not what you are saying?

A: Pediatricians are very conscious of what they say in these visits and how they say it. The most important thing to do is talk in terms of health and never weight loss. All of the words we use are around this sentiment, so we use terms like "vital signs" or "trends" and stay away from any alarming language. Another important thing to do is focus on the positive—what we can do to be healthier instead of what we need to stop doing.

From very early on, I talk to parents about "5-2-1-0"—five servings of fruit and veggies per day, two hours max of screen time, one hour of active time, and the zero stands for limiting things such as sugary drinks. This type of language should be ingrained at a young age so that at the teenage visit, this is not new or surprising information.

Q: I have heard too many stories about young women who come for a doctor visit just like this one but a year later have a full-blown eating disorder. It is not so much what the pediatrician is saying as much as it is what families and daughters do with the information once they go home. What advice do you have for families?

A: Conversations at these types of visits have two critical communication components: what the doctor is saying and hoping to convey in a thoughtful, delicate way, and what the daughter is hearing based on her life experiences—family dynamic, preexisting ideas of her body image, peer interactions. It's helpful to the doctor to know what the patient is bringing in to these visits.

Advice I would have for parents who have a doctor visit that brings up the concern for a high BMI is this:

1. Implement changes as a family. Your child is less likely to think there is something wrong with them if you solve the issue as a family unit instead of putting responsibility on the child. You are in this together. That means the entire

family eats out less, the entire family switches to whole grain pasta, the entire family limits sugary drinks.

2. Never use the word *diet*. You will never hear a pediatrician use this word and that is for a reason. Diets focus on weight loss, but our true concern is health. Shift always to the positive instead of the negative.

3. Implement changes slowly. You don't need to make all the changes at once. Often, I like to brainstorm with families as to one area at a time they can work on as a family. That way it is less overwhelming to the child.

4. Know your child. It is very important to know and assess your child's risk factors for eating disorders or disordered eating before going into a lifestyle change.

Q: Sometimes as a mom I feel I have to make a choice between their physical health and their emotional health. On the one hand, I need to enforce healthy eating to protect them from long-term physical health concerns. But on the other hand, if she takes what I say in the wrong way, I am putting her at risk for long-term insecurity and body image issues, which could possibly lead to eating disorders. How do I assess these choices?

A: Let's say you have one hundred girls with a high BMI. Out of those one hundred girls, a small percentage also has a high risk of developing an eating disorder. It is important that both the parent and the doctor assess these risks in advance of communicating to the daughter about a BMI concern.

Disordered eating risk factors include:

1. Your daughter has a high achieving, highly driven, and perfectionistic personality. In addition, you can take into consideration whether the temperament of the entire family leans toward high achievement, which can be

experienced as a lot of pressure. Young women with this type of personality can be much more likely to develop an eating disorder because they will take healthy lifestyle changes to an extreme.

2. Your daughter has already said things like "I am fat," or you can tell that she sees herself in a distorted way.

3. Your daughter's social media feed is full of images of people with highly fit bodies. Studies have shown that repeatedly viewing images like this greatly affects the way we see ourselves.

4. There is a family history of eating disorders. While there are currently not enough studies to prove that this may be a risk factor, it should be taken into consideration if Mom, Aunt, or Grandma had an eating disorder.

Q: If we have a daughter with a high BMI and all those risk factors, what should we do?

A: You do not mention BMI until you are sure it is safe to address. Focus instead on healthy nutrition and lifestyle in a routine way. I have had parents slip me notes. Sometimes the note says, "Please bring up healthy eating," and sometimes it says, "Please *do not* bring up BMI or healthy eating." It is important for us as doctors and parents to know our patient and not over-focus on weight and BMI if we think there is a risk they will not be able to safely handle the information. Often it is a good idea to stay "under surveillance" with the doctor. Instead of coming in once a year, you come in twice a year. This way the doctor can help you assess when and if it is a safe time to address lifestyle changes.

Q: I have a crazy theory I'd like to tell you. Please tell me what you think. As parents, it is our responsibility and most beneficial for our children to spend the first ten to eleven years of their lives teaching them healthy habits—healthy eating, being active, and so on. Then when they hit adolescence, we shift to concentrating our parenting efforts on their emotional and spiritual health, putting down our need to constantly tell them what to eat and what not to eat. What do you think?

A : I actually agree with that and it mirrors what they teach at the American Academy of Pediatrics. Development of healthy eating and healthy lifestyle begins at the first-year checkup. From the child's earliest checkups, we aim to partner with parents to start healthy eating habits young. If a child develops a weight issue, most often it is not the child's fault, and it is unfair to put unreasonable expectations on adolescent children.

If we are diligent to help a family implement good nutritional habits and healthy lifestyles when their children are young, we can often prevent overburdening the children with dramatic changes when they become adolescents.

Q : You are so right about that; adolescence can be so hard on our girls. But the best thing we can do is be aware of who our daughters are and be intentional with them. Which leads me to my last question. What would you say to the mom who thinks her daughter has a weight problem, but a doctor has never communicated that at any checkup?

A : If you see a doctor you trust, a doctor you have trusted to prescribe the right medicine when your child got sick, a doctor who has helped you diagnose asthma, for example, or other ailments, then you should absolutely 100 percent trust your doctor to raise concerns about BMI only when and if it is necessary. Pediatricians will only bring up health concerns if they are actually an issue, so if the doctor does not bring it up, you can take that as a signal that all is well.

Confident Mom
CHALLENGE

There are many battle references in the Bible. God's Word constantly reminds us not only that there is a war going on but also that we are the soldiers called to fight in it. Any picture of war is not a pleasant one. But opting out of the fight is not an option; if we want to win, we need to fight.

Challenge #3: Claim your battle. Name it! Decide what you are battling for. What specifically do you hope for your daughter, and are you willing to do anything to fight for it? For example, maybe you hope your daughter will finally see herself as beautiful just the way she is. Are you ready to fight to model that for her? Or maybe your prayer for your daughter is that she stays true to who she is instead of following those around her. Are you ready to help teach her to find her God-centered identity? Maybe you just want her to *love* her body instead of hating it. Are you willing to love yours first? Whatever it is for you, it might help to declare a battle verse. Take up your Bible and hunt for verses about the battle you are in. Choose one, talk about why you chose that verse, and display it somewhere in your home as a visual reminder to be on guard. Here are some possible references if you need a cheat sheet: 2 Corinthians 10:2–5; Ephesians 6:10–18; 1 Timothy 1:18; 6:12; 2 Timothy 4:7.

Bonus Challenge: Find out who or what else is fighting for your daughter. Pray for God to guard your own heart and check out Instagram, Facebook, or Twitter and peer into your daughter's world. What is battling for her heart there? What parts of her are her social media feeds fighting for?

Confident Daughter
DISCUSSION QUESTIONS

1. What are some of the pressures you face when you walk out your door? Be specific.

2. Name a woman who is your role model. What is it about her you admire?
3. Do you enjoy being alone in your room? Why or why not?
4. Who is the smartest person you know? What makes them someone you think you want to listen to or follow?
5. Do you think people are growing up too fast? Why or why not?
6. Who is someone in your life you would do anything for?
7. One of the best weapons of war that we have is God's Word. What are some of your favorite Bible verses? Why do you like them so much? If you don't have any, the Psalms or the book of John are great places to start.
8. Read Ecclesiastes 2:11 and Proverbs 3:21–22. What stands out to you about these verses?

A Mom's Prayer

Lord, help us have the courage and the wisdom to reach our girls, to reach our daughters. Lay on our hearts the right path to take. When we don't know what to do, will you guide us? When we don't know what to say, will you speak to us? When we don't know how to love her the way she needs to be loved, will you show us? This burden seems too heavy to bear. The road seems too long and difficult. But we will not be dismayed or discouraged. We know that you desire great things for our daughters. Do in us a great work. Amen.

Mirror, Mirror on the Wall

L et's just mic drop in chapter 4, shall we?

Ready. Set. Go.

You *are* right. You aren't as physically beautiful as Jezebel in your workout class. And your neighbor down the street? The one you obsessively watch on Instagram every morning while you are still in your flannel nightgown? Yep, her too. She is more physically beautiful than you.

You want to know what's even worse? That girl in your daughter's class, Sally Jo, you know, the one your daughter cries about because "I will never be as pretty as her!" You got it, she actually is physically prettier than your daughter.

On the flip side, there are just as many people whom you would beat on the "pretty scale" (according to a physiology paper I did on beauty in college, *pretty* includes facial symmetry, smooth complexion, and lack of physical imperfections). Same goes for your daughter; she might not be prettier than Sally Jo, but that doesn't mean she isn't pretty.

Why do we pretend that there are not varying degrees of beauty? Why do we deny this fact of life with our cliché thoughts and answers, telling ourselves or our daughters, "No! You are just as pretty as she is!"? Has hearing those words ever helped you? Or how about this one: "Beauty is on the inside, honey, don't worry about it." This statement is only half true. Yes, the Bible is clear that *true* beauty is not physical beauty at all. But we do ourselves and our daughters a vast disservice by pretending physical beauty is nothing when it is, in fact, very real and created by God.

Can we just sit in the discomfort of this reality for a minute? Together, can we grieve this, admit it, and seek healing from our trampled expectations?

Ladies, we will never be perfect, and neither will our daughters. And no matter what we do, say, eat, crunch, or tuck, we will never become beautiful enough to fix our confidence problem. There will *always* be someone prettier. Our only hope is healing from the inside out.

I realize this is uncomfortable. It is uncomfortable for me too. I remember a place and time that whenever I saw physical beauty I wanted to cry. I would even size up my friends and mentally decide if I were better off or worse off than they were. It was a terrible way to live. I felt the weight of it constantly—that my physical beauty would *never be good enough to make me feel good enough.* I imagine that your daughter could be living in a similar place.

But there is a different place for our minds to live. I've found this place. Through God's Word, his Holy Spirit, and a big dose of miraculous reality, I live there now. My prayer is that by the end of this book, you will live there too. But we have a hard shell to crack through, don't we? We must retrain our minds to think differently so that our words and our actions reflect this new place we live in.

Let's start on the banks of the ocean. It is early in the morning, and the sun has not yet risen. You sit there, your daughter is with you, and (since we are dreaming here) she is in your arms snuggled up next to you. The sun begins to rise, and the sky fills with the most beautiful colors you have ever seen. Pinks, oranges, yellows, and your breath stops just for a minute. *It's gorgeous.* It's heaven come to earth. You hold your daughter a little tighter, and you swear you can see angels in those clouds. You carry the vastness of God's creation with you for the rest of the day, and you ponder his endless creativity.

My dears, do we then desire to become the sun? Downcast, do our shoulders droop in sadness that we will never bear the colors of the sky?

Heavens no! Why would we? We were not created to be the sun.

Neither, then, were we created to be *someone else*. We are God's masterpiece. The colors we bear are ours alone—our curves, our parts, our imperfections, and our gloriousness belong only to us. Why do we spend a lifetime trying to change the unique sunrise that God has created in us? I imagine it makes God sad that we are not pleased with his canvas. That we resent the colors he chose to paint in us, and we smudge or try to color over what he has created. We are going to spend a few chapters talking specifically about how to stop trying to change ourselves and why we must if we are going to teach our daughters confidence. But for now, I would like us to sink into this question: Can the physical beauty God has given us be enough?

Can it begin to be enough? As we go through life, may we live as if we are constantly sitting on the shore. When we behold a physically beautiful woman or a physically handsome man, may we praise God for the amazing sunrise he created in them. May we appreciate the vastness of God's creativity and then may we *move along*. "Thank you for that beautiful sunrise of a person. Amen and Amen." Period.

Our obsession with physical beauty ends here in chapter 4. It has to. We must learn how to let it go if we are to know how to guide our girls. When they are gawking and crying and feeling down because their physical beauty doesn't match up, telling them "you are just as beautiful blah blah blah" or "you are the prettiest girl to mommy and daddy blah blah" or "honey, being beautiful on the inside is what counts blah" are just hollow words if we don't have anything to back them up. Or (even worse) if we don't really believe what we are saying. Or (way worse) we don't believe them about ourselves first.

Let's go live somewhere else, shall we? Let's pack up our emotions, trash our old baggage, and go shopping for a new perspective.

Biblical Beauty

Some women in the Bible are noted as being extraordinarily beautiful. Sarah, Rebekah, Bathsheba, and Esther are a few examples of those whom Scripture mentions as having physical beauty as one of their attributes.

Abraham pretended to be Sarah's brother because he feared that foreign leaders would kill him in order to take his beautiful wife (Gen. 12:12). When we first meet Rebekah, we read, "The woman was very beautiful" (Gen. 24:16). Bathsheba, well, you know about Bathsheba, and Esther won the beauty contests of all beauty contests! "Esther won the favor of everyone who saw her" (Esther 2:15). From these few examples, we can determine these truths: physical beauty is a gift that some have been given, and we have not all been given the same level of this gift.

We are not all meant to be the same; this we know and say. But do we talk about beauty this way, or do we try to even the playing field? When we watch the Olympics, do we think we too need to become elite athletes in curling, volleyball, hockey, or swimming? No! We admire their talent and their giftedness, we stand in awe of what the human body is capable of, and we move along with our day.

Friends, from now on let's pretend that there is an Olympics for physical beauty. Most of us are not in them, and that's okay because God has given us other gifts and we have important things to do. Let's not waste another minute trying to become an elite athlete in something we were not made for. May we teach our daughters to do the same.

In order to give up once and for all our obsession with trying to become more physically beautiful, let's first consider it biblically, and then we can hash it out practically.

I like lists, don't you? I found a list in the Bible that you might be interested in. It talks about the kind of beauty that we *do want to obsess over and aim for.* This kind of beauty we can grow in and fully achieve. Let's pray we can model this kind of beauty for our daughters, as it is much more important than beauty in any other form.

> A wife of noble character who can find?
>   She is worth far more than rubies.
> Her husband has full confidence in her
>   and lacks nothing of value.
> She brings him good, not harm,
>   all the days of her life.
> She selects wool and flax
>   and works with eager hands.
> She is like the merchant ships,
>   bringing her food from afar.
> She gets up while it is still night;
>   she provides food for her family
>   and portions for her female servants.
> She considers a field and buys it;
>   out of her earnings she plants a vineyard.
> She sets about her work vigorously;
>   her arms are strong for her tasks.
> She sees that her trading is profitable,
>   and her lamp does not go out at night.
> In her hand she holds the distaff
>   and grasps the spindles with her fingers.
> She opens her arms to the poor
>   and extends her hands to the needy.
> When it snows, she has no fear for her household;
>   for all of them are clothed in scarlet.

She makes coverings for her bed;
    she is clothed in fine linen and purple.
Her husband is respected at the city gate,
    where he takes his seat among the elders of the land.
She makes linen garments and sells them,
    and supplies the merchants with sashes.
She is clothed with strength and dignity;
    she can laugh at the days to come.
She speaks with wisdom,
    and faithful instruction is on her tongue.
She watches over the affairs of her household
    and does not eat the bread of idleness.
Her children arise and call her blessed;
    her husband also, and he praises her:
"Many women do noble things,
    but you surpass them all."
Charm is deceptive, and beauty is fleeting;
    but a woman who fears the Lord is to be praised.
Honor her for all that her hands have done,
    and let her works bring her praise at the city gate.
      (Prov. 31:10–31)

If we must stew on beauty, may we stew on these. When our daughters fret, may we teach them what godly beauty looks like with full love, power, and confidence. Here is the *true beauty* list:

Beauty of character is worth more than all the money in the world.

True beauty is confidence.

True beauty is putting others above ourselves.

True beauty is working hard.

True beauty is providing for others.

True beauty is learning a craft or business.

True beauty is using our bodies as they were meant to be used—for strong work.

True beauty is getting the job done.

True beauty is being generous to the poor and those who have less than we do.

True beauty is having no fear of the future, because we know God will be with us.

True beauty is hanging out with people of strong character.

True beauty is being responsible with money.

True beauty has strength.

True beauty has dignity.

True beauty is laughter.

True beauty speaks wisdom.

True beauty watches over others.

True beauty receives praise with grace and humility.

True beauty is noble.

True beauty knows that physical beauty fades.

True beauty trusts the Lord above all else.

True beauty is you.

As I pray over these verses and descriptions, I notice a huge difference between physical beauty and true inner beauty. True beauty is our choice. Isn't it soothing to have control over something? It feels nice, actually.

Since birth I have not had control over my nose size, boob size, or body structure. Having given birth to five children, I know we come out of the womb in all different shapes and sizes. Today, our daughters wrestle with this out-of-controlness. It doesn't feel fair and it doesn't feel nice and frankly they want what *she* has. But what if every day we practiced *choosing to be beautiful*? What if in our homes and in our own lives, we and our daughters began to take control over the things of beauty that are ours to control?

As you were reading the descriptions based on Proverbs 31, were you picturing what this woman or girl would look like? I was, but not her physical appearance. I saw joy in her eyes, a smile on her lips, and a strong, bold stance. Her beauty radiated all over. I want to be that woman. I know you want to be that woman too, and I know your daughter wants to become that woman.

Becoming a woman of true beauty takes one baby step at a time; it does not happen in one giant leap. We begin by changing the direction we are walking in and then taking a step.

Baby steps, friends, but baby steps with our daughters. That is the beauty of this journey. It is not one we teach our daughters in word only but a journey we go on *with* them. Hand in hand, we acknowledge the difficult terrain, we talk honestly about the pain we are experiencing, and we figure this thing out together.

When the physical beauty talks come, when the "I'm not as pretty as her" tears fall, identify the fact that this is not something we can change. Our bodies and our scale of physical beauty have been given to us once, and though we can oscillate a bit back and forth, we will never be completely satisfied. There will always be someone better and always someone worse, and we wear ourselves out when we spend all our energy in the *physical* beauty department.

What if we put that effort aside? Let's get off the physical improvement plan and get on to the true beauty plan. Take the following quiz with your daughter. Circle the appropriate number: 0 means you never ever act that way and 5 means you act that way all the time.

I spend more time focusing on my godly beauty than my physical beauty.

0 . . . . 1 . . . . . . 2 . . . . 3 . . . . . . 4 5

I care more about my beauty of character than anything else about me.

0 . . . . 1 . . . . . . 2 . . . . 3 . . . . . . 4 5

I believe that true beauty lies in my confidence.

0 . . . . 1 . . . . 2 . . . . 3 . . . . 4 5

I am beautiful when I put others above myself.

0 . . . . 1 . . . . 2 . . . . 3 . . . . 4 5

I am beautiful when I work hard.

0 . . . . 1 . . . . 2 . . . . 3 . . . . 4 5

I am beautiful when I help meet needs.

0 . . . . 1 . . . . 2 . . . . 3 . . . . 4 5

I am beautiful when I try new crafts and skills.

0 . . . . 1 . . . . 2 . . . . 3 . . . . 4 5

I am beautiful when I use my body for strong work.

0 . . . . 1 . . . . 2 . . . . 3 . . . . 4 5

I am beautiful when I try my best to get the job done well.

0 . . . . 1 . . . . 2 . . . . 3 . . . . 4 5

I am beautiful when I am generous to the poor and those who have less than I do.

0 . . . . 1 . . . . 2 . . . . 3 . . . . 4 5

I am beautiful when I am fearless.

0 . . . . 1 . . . . 2 . . . . 3 . . . . 4 5

I am beautiful when I trust God with my future.

0 . . . . 1 . . . . 2 . . . . 3 . . . . 4 5

I am beautiful when I surround myself with other women of godly character.

0 . . . . 1 . . . . 2 . . . . 3 . . . . 4 5

I am beautiful when I am responsible with the money God has entrusted to me.

0 . . . . 1 . . . . 2 . . . . 3 . . . . 4 5

I am beautiful when I treat myself and others with dignity.

0 . . . . 1 . . . . 2 . . . . 3 . . . . 4 5

I am beautiful when I laugh.

0 . . . . 1 . . . . 2 . . . . 3 . . . . 4 5

I am beautiful when I speak wisdom.

0 . . . . 1 . . . . 2 . . . . 3 . . . . 4 5

I am beautiful when I lift others up.

0 . . . . 1 . . . . 2 . . . . 3 . . . . 4 5

I am beautiful when I receive praise with grace and humility.

0 . . . . 1 . . . . 2 . . . . 3 . . . . 4 5

I am beautiful when I am trustworthy.

0 . . . . 1 . . . . 2 . . . . 3 . . . . 4 5

I am beautiful when I acknowledge that physical beauty fades, but beauty of character lasts forever.

0 . . . . 1 . . . . 2 . . . . 3 . . . . 4 5

I am beautiful when I trust the Lord above all else.

0 . . . . 1 . . . . 2 . . . . 3 . . . . 4 5

I am beautiful when I can say out loud that I am beautiful simply because I am me.

0 . . . . 1 . . . . 2 . . . . 3 . . . . 4 5

Every quality that you circled a 3 or below on, spend a day focusing on nothing but that quality. Do it together! For example, say your daughter circles a 1 for "I am beautiful when I use my body for strong work." Grab a day and use your bodies for strong work together. Or say you circled 2 for "I am beautiful when I laugh." Then go somewhere to laugh together!

Now that we have hammered this point home, I need to say to you that though we may not be the *most* beautiful, we most assuredly are each physically beautiful in our own ways. There is not an ugly soul walking this earth. God does not create ugly; when he made you, it pleased him greatly.

Playing the Hand We Have Been Dealt

Through the years, I have wrestled with the question of how much of our physical beauty we should allow others to see. A few years ago I wrote a mildly controversial blog post titled "The Problem with the Bikini Debate." In it I discussed that the real problem is not the bikini but the heart behind the bikini. Are we wearing a bikini or some other article of clothing to receive affirmation from others? Do we *need* to wear these clothes because we are unhealthily dependent on attention to our body? Are our daughters jaunting out of the house in booty shorts because a look from a boy in *that* way is better than no look at all? These are all heart issues and reveal deeper-level hurts that need to be addressed from the inside out. It's not the bikini as much as it is the story that the bikini is telling.

The debate and disagreement about the post came up when I talked about wearing a bikini with a different mindset. For example, the young girl who excitedly shared with me that she finally feels comfortable enough in her own skin to wear a bikini for the first time. Or the mom who shared that when she goes on vacation she loves to wear that *one* bathing suit because she knows it's her husband's favorite. Some felt uncomfortable with these options, but the point here is this: let's take the time to figure out *why* we wear what we wear and let's be intentional with our choices. Whatever you decide for you, for your daughter, for your home, go at it with prayer, with intention, and with joy.

We should give the same attention and consideration to our choices in regard to our makeup, our jewelry, and our wardrobe. Let's do this with purpose and share the process with our girls.

The question is not what is *she*, the one wearing the bikini, doing. The question is, What does God have for *me*?

I want to share with you my personal story about this but with one stipulation. This is an example, not a prescription. It is a testimony of a process, not a blanket statement of an end goal. My prayer is that you will do your own digging and soul searching with this question in mind: What do I want my daughter to learn from my "outward adornment" choices and philosophies?

Once upon a time (a long time ago, even though it feels like yesterday), I was months away from my wedding and sitting with a bunch of girlfriends. They were talking about plucking one's eyebrows. "What is that?" I asked. To my surprise, this was something women do, though I had never in my life removed a hair from anywhere on my face. Well, like good friends do, on the spot those ladies plucked my eyebrows. I felt like a whole new woman.

It took my fiancé a little while to look at me without thinking I was surprised all the time. All in all, we decided it was a fine thing for me to shape those eyebrows just a tiny bit. Who knew, right? Apparently, I was the only one who didn't know.

A few days later, I saw my sisters-in-law, and they said to me, "Thank goodness! We have been wanting you to do that for years!"

I'll let that soak in a minute. True story. Every word.

I wondered, *Why didn't somebody help a girl out sooner?* I'm fine with a few tips and tweaks along the way, and I had a rip-roaring time accepting the fact that I had lived with wonky (and very pluckable) eyebrows for the first twenty-two years of my life. I'm over it (eye roll), but the point is that my decision to pluck my eyebrows was no big deal. I liked getting to do a bit of a beauty routine, and it is fun to learn new things.

Same goes for me with clothes. Finally, at the age of thirty-five, I am beginning to allow myself to think I am important enough to wear clothes that fit correctly. I'm important enough to take the time to learn what styles are good for my body type and to buy something new every now and again. Juxtapose this to the old version of me who thought "I don't deserve it" or "it's not going to help anyway" or "nothing fits me right so why bother?" Rest assured, old Maria, there is a comfy pair of jeans and an adorable shirt for every shape and size. It's just a matter of taking the time to find them.

I have spent vast amounts of time (probably so much that my daughter is entirely sick of me) showing my daughter that makeup is fun but that I don't need it in order to leave the house. Faith has had an open door to makeup since she was little, and frankly she is entirely uninterested, but she watches me put it on often. I tell her that it is fun to try new colors and styles, and that it is kind of like painting a picture, but it is not the makeup that makes Mommy beautiful. It's Mommy that makes the makeup beautiful.

What is your story? What is your clothes style? Your body type? What clothes make you feel like Esther after her 365-day beauty routine?

What about your sweet girl? What is her body type? What stores would be best for her?

What about makeup? Can you go without it and still feel good? Does your daughter need to learn how to pluck her eyebrows? (Trust me, help a sister out!)

What about jewelry, handbags, belts? Fashion not your thing? No problem. Is it your daughter's? Do you need to step into her world and be interested?

I apologize for all the questions, but my desire is to earn your trust. When the Bible lays out a specific way as the best way, I promise I will tell you about it. If there are options, I want to give you the freedom to decide for yourself.

There is no option in this regard: tackle your honest view of physical beauty and align it with God's Word.

But figure out for yourself the hows, whens, whys, and whats that make you feel lovely. Figure it out with your daughter too (because feeling lovely is an important gift you want your daughter to have for herself).

From an Expert on Mirrors

Before I had my own children, I had sixty junior high students I called my own. They called me "Mama Maria"; I was theirs, and they were mine. I laughed with them, cried with them, and most importantly taught them all I knew about Jesus. Those girls? Those middle school girls I led? They were the girls who inspired me to write this book in the first place.

I heard their stories, I heard their cries, and I saw firsthand how a young girl is incapable of articulating the full weight of her struggle to her mom. I grabbed on to one group of girls in particular. Quinn and her friends were so adorable, so cute, so sweet, and so lovable, but I knew they saw none of these things in themselves. They were the girls passing on the chips when I thought they should share the whole bowl. They were the girls who couldn't quite get a handle on how to love themselves when I and the other adults in their lives knew there was so much there to love. I began writing this book ten years ago with the prayer that it might help minister to girls like Quinn and her friends.

Fast-forward a decade and guess who God sends back into my life? Quinn! One day she was reading her Holy Bible app and found a reading plan on fear based on a book called *Breaking the Fear Cycle*. She was struggling with fear over an old eating disorder rearing its ugly head again, and guess who God sent to love on her? The author of that book, Maria Furlough, her old youth leader.

Reconnecting with Quinn has been sweet, fun, and sad. It broke my heart to learn about the eating disorder she developed and how hard the journey to healing has been. I am sure she will be the first to tell you the journey is not over, but I am so honored to share a bit of her story with you. It is a story of hope. If God can bring Quinn peace in spite of that blasted mirror, there is hope for us too.

Q: Quinn, I know you have struggled with eating disorders. Can you share about what you used to see when you looked in the mirror?

A: I've always had trouble accepting the reflection I saw in the mirror. Every time I walked past my reflection, it would suck me in. I could spend hours in front of my bathroom mirror, picking apart every physical attribute I wanted to change. I saw all the other girls who I believed looked better than me. I saw their friends, I saw their happiness, and I saw how people acted around them. Maybe if I looked like them I could have more friends, more value, more purpose. I got sucked into that way of thinking in middle school, and my lack of self-confidence combined with various other issues and behaviors led me straight into a treatment center for eating disorders. I thought I had finally reached recovery after high school. I didn't engage in any eating disorder behaviors anymore (at least none that I considered dangerous); however, I would walk around my college campus and constantly compare myself to other girls. These girls were thin and pretty. Not only that, but they were on fire for God! They seemed so happy, so pretty, so perfect. I would go back to my dorm and spend more time looking in the mirror. My face was rounder, I had gained around fifteen pounds in college, but I didn't really care that much. I had an amazing boyfriend, a good work-study program, and seemed to be doing well in my classes. I got married after graduation, and all seemed well. Until I couldn't find a job.

My husband and I struggled to stay afloat while I searched endlessly for anyone who would take me. When I finally did find something, it was a work-from-home job that I didn't care for. After that, I began spending more and more time in front of the mirror. I couldn't find my value in my job anymore, so I turned to the mirror to define me. I hated what I saw. I lost a lot of weight and did everything outwardly to change my appearance, thinking that would make me happy. However, I was never satisfied with my reflection no matter how much I changed. That thought process and those behaviors landed me in another treatment center after ten years of recovery.

Q: You are an amazing woman of God. How did he help you to finally start seeing yourself the way he sees you?

A: God has been teaching me a lot about fixing my eyes on what is unseen instead of on what is seen (2 Cor. 4:18). I have spent so much time looking in the bathroom mirror instead of going out and living life! And I would have spent so much more time doing that if it wasn't for my amazing husband. You see, I came home from my six-week stay in an inpatient facility, went straight to the bathroom, and found that my husband had covered up the mirror with paper! I was ticked off at first, but then I saw his sweet note written on the paper. "I love you" and "you're beautiful" were scribbled across the parchment, and even though these notes were simple, they meant a lot coming from a person who I know doesn't necessarily wear his heart on his sleeve. That simple act from him has really freed up my time and my mind from focusing on what is seen. I have also spent each morning reading my Bible and journaling. Taking time to focus my mind on my loving Father every morning sets my heart in the right place to face the day ahead.

Q: What do you believe is most beautiful about you?

A: I've had a rough battle with self-hatred. I feel like I've had so many failures, and oftentimes I'll define my worth and my beauty from those failures. I've been working on self-acceptance and self-love, and man it's hard! However, I can finally say that there are beautiful things about me. I am a dedicated, hardworking, creative, and loving woman. I can finally accept that God has a different definition of beauty, and that truth in itself has transformed my life. God takes me just as I am, mess and all!

Q: What are some things that you have to do (or not do) in your life to protect your heart from focusing on your outer beauty instead of your God-centered beauty?

A: I have to work on consistency. Honestly, the chains of my eating disorder still grip me tightly. I struggle, but I know that I struggle with a purpose. I've already seen God use my story, and I have full confidence that he is able to bring complete healing to this chapter of my life. I still find that I compare myself to others, but I have tried to use that opportunity for prayer instead of comparison. Maybe if I pray for them, I will begin to see them as another person going through life instead of a marker against which I determine my worth. I know I have a long way to go, and I'm not exactly sure where I'm going at times, but I trust God to lead me.

Confident Mom
CHALLENGE

This challenge is the best one ever; it's a game changer, I promise! I pray you have the courage to do it and do it fully.

Challenge #4: Ditch the mirrors. All of them—in your whole house. Do we really need to look at ourselves so much? Keep a face mirror or two to brush your teeth and do your morning routine, but we don't need to see our bodies from every angle all the time. If God didn't give us eyes to see ourselves at that angle, then we don't need to see it! Be creative. Isn't Quinn's husband a gem? He covered up all the mirrors in the house with love notes to her (not a bad idea). Yes, I am positive your daughter might hate you for this at first, but it will be so worth it.

By loosening our grip on our mirrors, may we loosen our grip on the importance of our looks. Set a time goal: one week, thirty days. I ditched the full-length ones for good.

Bonus Challenge: Together with your daughter, print out Proverbs 31:10–31 in such a way as to cover an entire full-length mirror with God's definition of true beauty! Then put the mirror in a place where it can remind you often of what God's mirror looks like.

Confident Daughter
DISCUSSION QUESTIONS

1. Name someone who you think is more beautiful than you. Name someone who you think is less beautiful than you. How does it feel to say this out loud?

2. Can you find peace knowing that it's okay you are not perfect physically?

3. How do you feel when you are around people who are prettier than you? What can you do to handle these feelings?

4. Are there any parts of your body that you like (hair, nose, legs, boobs, arms)? Together with your daughter, name them. How does this process make you feel?

5. What makes you feel beautiful?

6. What are the beauty routines in your home? Are there any areas that need a God-centered improvement? Which ones and why?

7. Do you like clothes shopping? Why or why not? How can you help each other make clothes shopping fun?

8. Can you live without makeup? Why or why not?

9. Be honest: How much of your worth is tied up in how you look? Take a moment to pray for the strength to believe that God can work on this in you.

10. Look up Proverbs 31 and name the characteristics of a godly beautiful woman that you see in each other.

A Mom's Prayer

Father, we confess to you that we covet physical beauty. We see it all around us, and it seems like it would be an amazing thing to have. We think that if we were just a little bit prettier, we would not hurt as much. We tell you this, Lord, because we need you to heal us of this! And we want you to heal us so that you can equip us to heal our daughters too. We are sorry, Lord, that we have been chasing after the wind of physical beauty for too long. We desire greater things for our lives today. Help us to seek out the characteristics of true beauty. Give us your wisdom, and may the Holy Spirit give us all we need to model this well for our daughters. We pray that our sweet girls would loosen their grip on comparison. Instead, may we give them sweet places to land that make them feel lovely, beautiful, and whole just the way they are. Lord, as you know, this is no small thing, and we need your help. Come with us now, you who can do all things. In Jesus's name we pray. Amen.

five

A Moment on the Lips

*I*t's not about you and me.

Chatting about our personal choices will sound at first like it is about us, but it's not. It's about our daughters and God. May this be our mantra until the very end of these pages. May we seek first to know what wisdom in God's Word we can glean in hopes of helping our daughters with their insecurities. May we be honest with ourselves in assessing where our faith falls on the priority list of what we are modeling for our girls, and may we turn to one another in love and guidance. So here we go. May Jesus guide us as we venture into the *food zone*.

Come with me to January 1, 2018. Happy New Year! I had officially spent the last five weeks of my life eating *all the things* at Thanksgiving, Christmas, and New Year's, and all the cells in my body were screaming, "Stop eating cookies!"

"Okay, fine," I say. It's been awhile (like a decade) since I've tried to be on a diet, so let's give it another whirl. I look around, do an assessment of what everyone else is doing, and the Whole30 plan sounds fancy and fun. It's thirty days; what could go wrong? Out goes the sugar, the dairy, the grains, and anything processed, and for fourteen days I ate almost nothing but fruits and vegetables.

What I am about to say is not at all a stand against Whole30. I think if God wired you that way and it brings your life joy and wholeness, then you should go for it. But it wreaked havoc on my very heart, mind, and soul.

I shot right back to seventh grade. I became obsessed all over again with my jean size, the mirror, the scale, and calories. All the things I had fought so hard with God to gain control over, the battle to focus on him instead of fat content and calorie count—all went out the window in one fell Whole30 swoop. An old addiction rose up in me once more, and I couldn't believe it. One decade of godly confidence was threatened by fourteen days of dieting.

On day fifteen, I decided it wasn't worth it. My soul and my emotions could not handle what my body was doing. In had come the comparison, the body analysis, the feeling guilty over *every single bite*, and I knew it was time for me to stop. I had to mentally and spiritually detox myself from the dieting and weight loss, and I had to once more come to grips with why freedom in food is so important for my God-centered confidence.

A month later, I still found myself eating only a half slice of pizza for dinner and feeling guilty over any "unhealthy" bit of food, and finally I had had it! I had to do something drastic. I was so mad. Where had my perspective gone, and how did it leave so fast? It revealed to me something deeply concerning about my soul; it is intricately connected to my food choices, and Jesus and I had a long discussion that resulted in the following decision *for me*: *I, Maria Furlough, choose to have a larger waistline, bigger jean size, and higher number on the scale if it means freedom in my eating to not diet or count calories or concern myself 100 percent of the time with health content.*

This is my eating covenant with God, and it was something I *had to do in order to keep Jesus on the throne of my life.*

I most assuredly realized once more that the choices we make about food, the diets we choose to embark on, and the foods we choose to fixate on are more than just physical decisions. They impact our mind, body, and spirit, and we have to bring God into the equation. It's more than food. It's more than dieting. It's more than losing a few pounds. And if it is affecting us in this way, how much more do we need to protect our daughters' developing and growing minds!

Our girls notice every bite we take, every food choice we make. We are setting them up for their life, their womanhood, and our choices impact whether they will develop healthy eating habits or disordered eating habits. And not only healthy eating but also healthy in mind, body, and spirit—the *healthy* that looks like God's healthy.

An Honest Assessment of *Why*

There are two different ways we model eating in our home: what we do and what we provide. This is a no-judgment zone. You are free to provide whatever type of food in your home that you'd like. We are going to dig into God's Word about food shortly, but the Bible does not tell us that there is only one way to eat. In fact, it says the opposite. So whether your home is going to be a no-sugar zone or a donut-counts-as-breakfast zone is entirely, fully, and 100 percent up to you. There are one hundred million books that can help you in the decision-making process if you need it.

What this chapter is about is identifying the answer to these three questions:

Why do we choose the food we do?
How is it honoring God?
What is it teaching our daughters?

Let's just get the hard one done and over with. *Why do we choose the food we do?*

Honest truth? I feigned the fact that my diet was for health. Actually, I felt fat after the holidays and wanted to fix it fast with a crash diet instead of taking the long road of eating fewer cookies. It took some deep digging for me to admit this to myself. On the surface was the need to stop eating in excess; below the surface was an underlying addiction to control, looking put together, and trying to be the model citizen of a woman. What about you? Why do you choose what you choose? I won't tell anyone, I promise. Your secret is safe with me. This is an honest assessment between me, you, and God, and you don't have to tell a single soul. Dig deep with me and identify the answers to the following questions:

> Am I making this food choice because I want people to think I am amazingly self-controlled and healthy and awesome?
>
> Am I making this food choice because I have an obsession with my looks and sustaining them?
>
> Am I making this food choice because I have a fear of gaining weight?
>
> Am I making this food choice because my worth is tied up in my size or physical beauty?
>
> Am I making this food choice because healthy eating has become an idol in my home?
>
> Am I making this food choice because it is my main form of control?
>
> Am I making this food choice because I think more about food than anything else and I cannot get it off my mind?

Sisters, you are not alone in your answers. My answer has been yes to every single one of these questions at various times. When my answer to even one of them is yes, I need a heart check and I need to make an immediate change. Not tomorrow, not next week, not after I reach my desired jean size—I need to change *now*. My daughter's growth doesn't take a break. I don't have the luxury of taking my time to get my disordered eating in check. She is growing and watching and learning *now*. Today, on this day, together and with courage, may we take up eating food God's way.

God wants to be the answer to all of these issues. He reminds us gently in his Word that he does not see what we see. While we chase after these food accomplishments (or failures), he is waiting patiently for us to turn back to him.

In the Old Testament, God sent Samuel to the family of David to find the next king, but the Lord did not tell Samuel which brother was the one. Samuel saw David's brothers—strong, tall, strapping, and handsome—and he thought, *Surely, one of these will be the next king.* To this sentiment God says (and may it penetrate us to the core as we continue to learn together):

> Do not consider his appearance or his height, for I have rejected him. The Lord does not look at the things people look at. People look at the outward appearance, but the Lord looks at the heart. (1 Sam. 16:7)

May I shout it to the mountaintops, over and over again, as loud as I can and with all my heart and soul: GOD DOES NOT LOOK AT THE THINGS PEOPLE LOOK AT. Doctors, nutritionists, and weight loss specialists are part of the solution, but they are not the whole. The latest research is not the only source of truth we have. We must hold everything up to the Word of the Lord and ask ourselves, *What is the Lord seeing when he looks into my heart?*

Food God's Way

As my daughter, Faith, was growing up, she stood tall and proud that her favorite food was corn dogs.

Corn dogs. (I just gagged a little typing these words.) With every single bite she took, my mind would explode with all that I know about corn dogs. Words such as *intestines* and *mystery meat* and *triple fried* would flow through my mind, and I was

81

tempted to toss my mothering completely out the window. Is there any mothering failure greater than your daughter's favorite food being *corn dogs*?

But as I would challenge myself to move from my adult brain into her child's brain, I would find this truth at hand: for her, joy comes with the corn dogs. And for me, the only way I am stealing that kind of joy from my girl is if Jesus tells me to. If God's Word teaches me, in all its wisdom, that there are certain foods we are *never* ever to enjoy, then that is what I will teach my children. But the Bible doesn't say, "Thou shalt not eat corn dogs," so here is the next question: What *does* the Bible teach us about food?

As I type this, I am giddy. I just love when the Bible paves a way for us and we need not navigate on our own. Here we go, one chunk at a time.

> I am convinced, being fully persuaded in the Lord Jesus, that nothing is unclean in itself. But if anyone regards something as unclean, then for that person it is unclean. If your brother or sister is distressed because of what you eat, you are no longer acting in love. Do not by your eating destroy someone for whom Christ died. (Rom. 14:14–15)

Let's pause a minute to define some terms. The idea of clean and unclean food comes from a long historical context dating all the way back through the Old Testament. In the book of Leviticus, God lays out for his people strict rules about what to eat and not eat. Before Jesus came, their only way to *cleanliness* before God was following the law. Praise be to God that we do not live in that time, and neither did the audience to which Paul was writing this passage. Jesus says in Mathew 5:17, "Do not think that I have come to abolish the Law or the Prophets; I have not come to abolish them but to fulfill them."

The old law of clean and unclean had been fulfilled. No longer did these rules need to be followed; in the freedom of Christ, people now had the liberty to follow whatever rules of eating they chose. Do you choose to eat clean? Eat clean. Do you choose to eat foods once deemed unclean? Eat away. But in all of these matters, consider your fellow sisters and brothers in Christ.

Greater than anything else we can do for our daughters, our first purpose is to disciple them. Our sweet girls are still growing. Their minds and bodies are not as developed as ours. Their brains cannot fully comprehend the health benefits of food, and they can't yet separate emotion from logic (see the interview with a counselor in chap. 7 for the science behind this). Try as we might to teach them better, they have grown up in a culture and a world that links food choices to dress size. They are sponges, absorbing whatever food truths have been thrown at them. We need to be careful they are not being confused by what they see in their very own homes. We need to assess and take into serious consideration what we do so as to *not by our eating destroy someone for whom Christ died*.

In Paul's audience were people who were not able to separate their eating lives from their spiritual lives. Worrying about eating was keeping them from Jesus. I pray that in our homes, worrying about eating does not keep our girls from Jesus.

There is even more goodness in this next passage.

> Do not let what you know is good to be spoken of as evil. For the kingdom of God is not a matter of eating and drinking, but of righteousness, peace and joy in the Holy Spirit, because anyone who serves Christ in this way is pleasing to God and receives human approval.
>
> Let us therefore make every effort to do what leads to peace and to mutual edification. Do not destroy the work of God for the sake of food. All food is clean, but it is wrong for a person to eat anything that causes someone else to stumble. It is better not to eat meat or drink wine or to do anything else that will cause your brother or sister to fall. (Rom. 14:16–21)

As I read these words, I am immediately taken back to my years as a middle school youth director. I loved those kids like my own children, and I was acutely aware of where they were in their faith. I was also acutely aware of the fact that eyes were on me at *all* times.

Time and again I would hear these words from young women: "My mom says that carbs are bad, so I can't have that" or "I am on a diet; I won't eat that." The young girls who were taught to pass up cookies and snacks and chocolate watched me to see what I would do. This was the very first time I felt the weight of the example I carried. I loved them so deeply, and it broke my heart that at twelve and thirteen, while gathering with friends, all they could think of was the dos and don'ts of food. Even worse, I wept as I watched them fall into eating disorders at such young ages. I wanted better for them than I had in my youth. I wanted so badly for them to see that food does not need to control us. It doesn't need to be an enemy combatant and a constant source of stress. I wanted them to see Jesus.

During that season of life, I happened to be trying to lose weight. I was settling into my adult years and needed to figure out what balanced eating looked like, particularly as I was no longer a college student constantly playing sports. It was an enigma for me. I was confident that I was doing an okay thing by learning healthy eating for myself, but I was also confident that my call to faithfulness was to be a good model for these girls. What was I to do?

It was simple: love trumped every time. In each situation, love won. I ate the cookie, chose my favorite candy bar, or grabbed a few chips and continued on with my evening and laughed with them in full joy over our time together. So as to not let them spin further into the lies that plagued them, I put my own eating priorities aside. I did not binge on junk food in front of them but chose to unceasingly display moderation.

Jesus, help us not to be the source of stumbling in our homes! May righteousness, peace, and joy in the Holy Spirit be *the most present items in our kitchens.*

There Is a Solution: Treat Food Like You Treat Sex (Shh, It's Private)

I believe that this next verse in our Romans 14 study warrants a section all to itself: "So whatever you believe about these things keep between yourself and God" (Rom. 14:22).

I know what you're thinking. This verse says nothing about sex! No, it doesn't, but God has used this one little food and sex parallel to give me tangible ways to check myself when it comes to food modeling in my home.

I love this verse! What a gift God has given us; we have full freedom in our food choices. So whatever it is that you believe, you do that, but keep it "between yourself and God." In other words, keep your food talk like your sex talk: private and behind closed doors.

We are all grown up now. We have cholesterol checks, blood tests, and blah blah blah. Unfortunately, we cannot stop adulting when it comes to food. There will be seasons when we need to eat less, better, more, and different. So do it! Just keep it between you, God, and that faithful friend or spouse you always turn to for venting sessions. This doesn't mean we never talk about our struggles (or victories) with food or eating. Just as with the topic of sex, it is important to be open and honest and not travel this life alone. But we also don't need to bring it up at the family dinner table or in line at the women's brunch.

No, my daughter doesn't need to hear about intimate discussions my husband and I have, and she also doesn't need to hear about my current food season.

What does this look like?

When I was experiencing my fourteen days of Whole30 terror, I *refused* to let my children know. I didn't tell them about it, and when they offered me a few of their M&M'S, I took them. Don't judge me. I know it sounds lame, but guarding their hearts when it comes to food is of utmost importance to me, and I rise up like an angry momma bear if anyone even speaks about dieting in front of my children.

These are some examples of words and phrases I have cast out of our home and family:

I can't eat that; I am on a diet.

Mommy is trying to lose weight.

I am staying away from _____ [fill in the blank] right now.

Ugh, why did I eat that?

I ate too much; that's going to go straight to my thighs.

Have I thought all of these things? Um, yeah, pretty much every day. But those are my issues to take up with my Savior, who cares for me and wants me to bring my burdens to him. These struggles are not for the ears of my growing and impressionable children.

I was talking with a friend of mine the other day about the woes of having to make different food choices as our bodies age. I am in my midthirties, she is in her midforties, and she giggled as she told me, "Girl, enjoy it now! Once I turned forty it all went downhill fast!" This conversation between the two of us included both joking and being serious. There are certain foods that take care of our bodies and certain foods that damage them. You know what? As adults our brains have matured enough to be able to process these food truths logically and to separate healthy eating from weight loss. I don't care what I weigh anymore, but I do want to be strong and healthy for as long as I can be. Adolescents do not yet have the mental ability to separate their emotions from their decisions about food (or anything else for that matter).

The American Academy of Child and Adolescent Psychiatry states:

Pictures of the brain in action show that adolescents' brains work differently than adults when they make decisions or solve problems.

86

Their actions are guided more by the emotional and reactive amygdala and less by the thoughtful, logical frontal cortex. . . .

Based on the stage of their brain development, adolescents are more likely to:

- act on impulse
- misread or misinterpret social cues and emotions
- get into accidents of all kinds
- get involved in fights
- engage in dangerous or risky behavior

Adolescents are less likely to:

- think before they act
- pause to consider the consequences of their actions
- change their dangerous or inappropriate behaviors[1]

Two things stand out to me about these statements and, as a mother, cause me to pause for concern. First, the fact that adolescents are more likely to "misread or misinterpret social cues and emotions" tells me that any young woman who hears from a doctor, mother, friend, or aunt that "you need to probably eat more carrots and fewer chips" is not going to understand they are saying this so that she can be healthier. Even our best intentions for her long-term health will be misread as an attack on her body or size. The adolescent girl's brain hinders her from translating "healthy eating" to "healthy living" and instead (most often) translates "healthy eating" to "be skinnier." We live in a culture obsessed with stopping body shaming, yet we are 100 percent okay with encouraging a fourteen-year-old to pass on the cookies.

Second, the fact that adolescents are less likely to "change their dangerous or inappropriate behaviors" reminds me that twice in the past year I heard of the sad stories of young women around the age of thirteen going to the doctor for a yearly well visit. Because of a slightly high BMI and weigh-in, both young women were advised to lose a few pounds. By the end of the year, both girls were hospitalized for eating disorders. What started out as a good intention to listen to their doctor and eat healthier ended in an eating disorder. Why is this a risk that we are willing to take? Why are we so willing to save their bodies at the expense of their spirit, emotions, and mind? It's not okay. I believe we have to hear studies like this about adolescents' developing brains and apply what we learn from them to what we say, do, teach, and model about eating. Our daughters' brains are not yet able to separate emotion from reason, and there is nothing more emotional for a young woman than her body.

From an Expert on Nutrition

Angela Wilkinson is one of those women—you know who I am talking about. God must have broken the mold when he made her type because she is physically perfect, every inch tight, and with a smashing smile to match. Of course, I am positive Angela would not agree, and that is why we are going through this book together. Right? Right.

To top it all off, Angela is the proud president and founder of the very successful nutrition company Total Nutrition Technology (TNT) in Charlotte. We have known each other for years, but when we got the opportunity to go on a mission trip together, my body image and insecurity eyes and ears were on high alert. I was watching her. *How would she treat food? How would she talk about food?*

She probably didn't even know she was being watched. What appeared before me was a godly woman who runs her company God's way. I noticed she was never "too good" to eat what everyone else was eating. This encouraged me that it is possible to be healthy without always going to extremes. When I finally got to share with her about the content of this book, it was like fireworks went off. How refreshing it was to hear her healthy perspective on food. I want to share a bit of it with you straight from Angela. She has multiple certifications and degrees on nutrition. Here it is—the perspective of a godly nutrition expert.

Q: What is disordered eating, and how does it differ from an eating disorder?

A: Many people can have disordered eating. It is not an eating disorder but follows many of the signs such as weight obsession, weight fluctuation, yo-yo dieting, preoccupation with weight and body, and irregular eating behaviors. None of these are to the extreme that they warrant a diagnosis of a specific eating disorder, but they certainly can be unhealthy for us. This is very common among our population, males as well as females.

Q: Angela, many of us have heard of anorexia, bulimia, and binge eating, but can you explain what orthorexia is?

A: Orthorexia is the desire to consume *only* healthy foods and causes a person to give up his or her normal lifestyle. Instead of caring about providing the adequate amount of nutrients for the body, they are preoccupied with worries about what might constitute the healthiest food. A healthy diet should have a positive impact on health and, at the same time, not affect relationships with other people or the quality of life and emotional states.

Q: I love that because I completely agree; healthy eating should not impact our relationships. Especially the most important ones like our relationship to our daughters. Can you talk a little about the importance of the mother-daughter relationship when it comes to food?

A: Yes. Mothers and parents are the role models; kids are watching even when we don't think they are. In fact, there is a strong tie-in with a mother's self-esteem and body image and the daughter's. So what can we as moms do? Be that great role model; our words and actions are so powerful (this is scriptural too). We need to love our bodies as a woman/mom and treat our bodies with love and respect and care. I think it is so important to use positive affirmations daily: look at yourself in the mirror, eye to eye, and quote Scripture out loud.

Q: Angela, so many moms are concerned that their daughters are going to develop poor eating habits, not make healthy eating choices, and/or gain weight. How can we help our daughters with these without damaging their confidence and possibly putting them at greater risk for an eating disorder?

A: Teach them how to be intuitive eaters. We are all born with intuitive eating habits, but through time society teaches us not to trust our mind-body connection. Allow our daughters to trust their tummies. As a parent, it is our job to provide and introduce to our children well-balanced and healthy food choices but allow them to decide how much to eat of what. It's a scary step for some of us moms who want full control! But if we are too restrictive or controlling, our efforts will backfire. We can offer new foods and encourage our kids to try different healthy foods but don't hyperfocus on that. Because, guess what, if our kids want junk food they will find a way to eat junk food (like at a friend's house or when they finally get their driver's license and hit a fast-food restaurant, because they can)!

Confident Mom
CHALLENGE

Challenge #5: Write down any "rules" you have about eating and then challenge yourself to go one week without thinking about them. It might take a little while to settle into—we have lived with these rules for so long—but try looking at food as a blank slate. Eat when you are hungry the food that God has blessed you with and made available to you—no more and no less than this.

Bonus Challenge: If Jesus can find joy in eating, then so can we! Make a date with your daughter that is food based (a tea time, a dinner, a breakfast), and practice savoring every bite, enjoying one another's company, thanking God for the provision of food, and letting go of any temptation to calorie count or control.

Confident Daughter
DISCUSSION QUESTIONS

1. How do you feel about food—do you love it or hate it? Why?
2. Does food make you feel guilty or free?
3. On a scale of 1 to 10, how important are food choices at home? How much do you talk about them? In comparison, on a scale of 1 to 10, how important is God in your home? How much do you talk about him?
4. Do you struggle with disordered eating? Is this an area that you would consider giving over to God and allowing him to heal?
5. Mom, do you have any unhealthy attitudes toward food that you would like to seek your daughter's forgiveness for?
6. Daughter, do you have any unhealthy attitudes toward food that you would allow your mom to help you defeat?
7. Based on the verses in Romans 14 shared in this chapter, what are some ways we can protect each other from stumbling in our faith in regard to food?
8. Is food (healthy eating or unhealthy eating) on the throne in your house? In other words, what holds the most important place of honor in your home? Is there anything that needs dethroning?

A Mom's Prayer

Father, thank you for the freedom you have given to us and thank you that Jesus came to set us free! Would you help us to live fully in this freedom? We confess to you that our treatment of food gets muddled with our own insecurities and sins, and we pray for your forgiveness and guidance. Above all else, Lord, we pray that you would be at the center of our kitchens and pantries. May our daughters grow free—free from disordered eating, free from seeing food as an enemy, and free from carrying a burden too heavy for their sweet and growing shoulders. Would you protect them from this, Lord, and would you use us—their mothers—to show them what free and confident living looks like? Amen.

six

Let's Get Physical

*E*ven now, as I write these words, I am struggling deeply with this chapter. I have written and rewritten it several times, deleting full sections after spending hours writing them.

Why? Because the line between worship of physical fitness and finding pure joy in it is thin and vague, yet how *we* treat our bodies teaches our daughters so much. I wrestle because I myself toggle between right and wrong motives. I am caught in the adult condition of aging, and I know if I don't use my God-given muscles I will grow weak. But I must fight the teenager in me that obsesses over toning, losing weight, and being in better shape than I am today.

As you read this chapter, please extend grace to me, knowing full well that my heart is not to cast judgment or to condemn but to figure this thing out together.

Our culture is doing a deep dive right now, making physical fitness nothing short of a god. Those in the best shape ascend to the top tier of our society. If you aren't beating your body into shape, you better start soon.

Is this truly what God wants for us? Is this truly what he wants us to give our best passion, most time, and greatest pondering to?

This is a good time to remind ourselves that this book is not about us, and together we acknowledge that being an adult is not easy. We face health trials of many kinds and may even have found ourselves in front of a doctor who says, "You need to spend more time being physically active." I get that, and I am not suggesting we ignore our doctor's advice. But we have to learn that an adult's need or desire to be in better physical shape does not translate well into the developing minds of our girls.

They are *not* adults yet. They are not yet caught in the adult condition of aging. They are *growing*. Though their bodies are getting there, and their hormones constantly tell them that they are, their brains and bodies are not yet fully developed.

Consider this from an article in *Pediatrics & Child Health*:

Concern with weight and shape is extremely common during the adolescent years. In addition to being exposed to the very real health risks of obesity and poor nutrition, teenagers are being exposed to the unrealistically thin beauty ideal that is portrayed in the media. Unfortunately, this overemphasis on the importance of being thin is internalized by youth who equate thinness with beauty, success and health. Through media exposure, teenagers are also exposed to a number of ways to lose weight and achieve this thin ideal. The sources of information available on health and nutrition are often dubious and unreliable, motivated less by scientific evidence than by fad trends and financial incentives. The net result is that many teenagers feel the cultural pressure to be thinner than is required for good health.[1]

The question for us is, Are we fighting this thin ideal or feeding it?

We can teach our daughters to look out into the world and call out a lie when they see it. We can remind them every day that they do not need to strive for skinny, or thin, or perfect, or tone, but our words are like dust in the wind if that is what they see us do when they look at our lives. If I say to my daughter, "Striving toward beautiful is not for you, sweet child, because you are beautiful just the way you are," and she watches me obsessively hammering it out in the gym every week in order to "keep in shape," then my words are a resounding gong. They are not filled with truth and real-life examples of my own confidence to back up what I am saying to her.

If we are going to talk the talk of God-centered beauty and fight off the thin ideal of the world, then we had better walk the walk. I say this with the understanding that this is a long and hard uphill battle. I see it in my Bible studies and meetings; we share our latest gym stories and the woes of working out. In the gym, the word *result* is placed on every banner and held high in our hearts and motivations. So for this time that we are spending together for the sake of our girls, let us too aim for results—in us, in our homes, and most importantly in our daughters.

The result of confidence despite current body size.

The result of believing in and living in God's definition of beauty.

The result of victory over the world's ideals and passions.

The result of standing firm even when everyone else is falling.

The result of giving our daughters firmly to Jesus every day and trusting he will equip us when we ask him to.

Yes, these are the results I want to fight for.

As guests walk into my local gym, we are greeted by a sign that reads, "If it doesn't challenge you it won't change you."

Preach, gym sign, preach! As we dig into this chapter, may we remember those words. Let the challenging and changing begin.

Back to Jiggly Arms

Once a week I find myself with the opportunity to attend a class at our local gym. My youngest son loves his time in child watch, and any excuse to put off the laundry that awaits me at home is welcome. So every Tuesday we head in.

I love entering into my forty-five minutes of sanity. It clears my mind and it resets my ever-increasing hormonal imbalances. Also I (secretly) like pretending I am a Marvel superhero training for my next battle. Victory must be won! It's one of my happy places, one of the few hours per week I allow myself to have guilt-free me time.

One class in particular sticks in my mind. Every once in a while, we need to grab a partner for an exercise, and there was a young woman in class with me whom I loved to work with. I had grown particularly fond of her, and I always jetted right to her for partner time. She was joyful, she worked hard, and her pace pushed me. After all, the world hangs in the balance (ahem, remember superhero training).

One day we got to chatting about our particular hatred of a certain set of exercises, to which she said to me, "I hate them, but, ya know, I have *got* to try to get rid of these jiggly arms!" (Insert a picture of her holding up an arm and flicking the hanging part back and forth and back and forth.) Apparently, jiggling arms are following me through life.

I could not get the picture of her jiggling arm out of my mind, and I became so sad as I realized the reality of the situation we are in. We care so much. We care too much, and we hate too many pieces of ourselves. We don't see strong, capable, or worthy; instead, we see jiggly, flabby, or large. We don't feel grateful for or happy about our pieces. No, most of the time we hate them, and (if we are being honest) the reason we are at the gym is to change said pieces.

What has happened to us?

Really, who gives a flying flip if our arms jiggle? Why does it matter if we have cottage cheese thighs? Where did we get the notion that any body part with fat on it is bad, and why do we fixate on it? Are our lives really over if we can never change our "trouble spots"? So what if we don't look perfect naked? Who does this really impact? I am serious here.

I spent the early years of my life actually believing that deleting any fat I had on my body was the holy grail of accomplishment. We are at risk of teaching our daughters the same exact thing. If we could just whip our bodies into a certain shape, then all the other aspects of our lives would fall into place. Magazines and health experts yell at us on a regular basis: "You have to work out at least thirty minutes a day, three days a week, in order to achieve the body you desire." You know what these standards do to our hearts, our confidence, our daughters' maturing minds? They give us a label, which runs the risk of haunting us for years: failure.

Jiggly arms? Failure.

Protruding butt? Failure.

Cottage cheese thighs? Failure.

Haven't been to the gym today? Failure.

Haven't worked out this year? Triple failure.

Don't even know what Burn Boot Camp is? Quadruple failure.

But there is good news. Today we stand with the potential for victory easily within our grasp. God came to heal the failures. God came so that our failures would be paid for once and for all.

You know what I want for my daughter and for your daughters, your friends' daughters, and your neighbors' daughters down the road? I want them to not even notice jiggly arms. I want them to be so fixated on what's truly important that they aren't concerned about the jiggly arm issues of their mothers. That is why we are in this book together, because we know we have fallen short for years, and we want the better way for our girls. We believe that God is powerful enough to make this permanent change in us.

Our bodies carry purpose, they carry importance, and each part is uniquely equipped with a certain set of skills. May we focus on this. May we rest here until the thoughts stop coming that our bodies are only for *looking at* and *shaping up*. Superheroes unite! We have work to do.

Of Some Value

Our girls are keen. They are in the world, they are on social media, they hear and see all sorts of things, and they wonder how their moms will react to it all. They don't tell us they do this. They are too busy acting miserable and like they hate us. They don't tell us they are actually modeling their lives after us. But whether they realize it or not, they are. And they will learn good and bad from us. We need to know this and prepare.

My mom. My sweet mom. A *thank you* to my mom for allowing me to unveil my youth, even when it involves leg crunches in the hallway, in the hopes and prayers that it helps mothers and daughters out there who need it. Thank you for allowing me to tell our story.

Ahem, as I was saying, leg crunches in the hallway.

Most mornings as I was getting ready for school, I walked out of my bedroom and *stepped over* my mom, who was doing leg crunches in her underwear in the middle of our hallway. You know the kind. Lying on one side, elbow on the ground, leg up and down, up and down, hitting that "trouble spot" in hopes that one magical morning it would be gone. "One and two and three and four," switch sides, and "one and two and three and four."

My heart broke in half. I knew my mom hated her thighs. I knew I was destined to hate mine too. I also knew that no amount of leg crunches was going to miraculously change the facts. Thus spun the icky vicious cycle of working out *for all the wrong reasons*.

You may not be doing leg crunches in your hallway, but what does your daughter hear you saying about physical activity? What does she observe you doing? What level of obsession (or hatred) toward physical activity do you communicate in your home?

Remember, they don't need to actually *hear* anything from you on the topic. They watch you, and so they know. May our sights be so set on a greater hope that we spare them from workout obsessions (or hatreds) and leg crunches in the hallway.

If it's a family hobby? If your daughter loves being physically active so much that she wants Mom to come along for the ride, awesome. It falls right in line with strawberry picking, horseback riding, festival going, and (if it floats your boat) CrossFit training.

It's fun. It brings joy. It brings laughter. It brings unity. All the rest falls away.

How does the rest fall away? Exactly what kind of perception shift are we talking about?

May we set our sights for a little while on the one form of truth that we can take to the bank. Scripture says this:

> Have nothing to do with godless myths and old wives' tales; rather, train yourself to be godly. For physical training is of some value, but godliness has value for all things, holding promise for both the present life and the life to come. This is a trustworthy saying that deserves full acceptance. That is why we labor and strive, because we have put our hope in the living God, who is the Savior of all people, and especially of those who believe. (1 Tim. 4:7–10)

I love the context that J. Vernon McGee gives about this passage:

> Paul's emphasis on godliness rather than physical exercise is because the Ephesians were a people given over to games and athletics. We are also that kind of a nation. Many of our cities have coliseums where great spectacles are conducted, and many believers put more emphasis on athletics than they do on the things of God. There are church officers who spend more time during the summer in the ball park than they spend in prayer meetings. Paul is not saying bodily exercise is wrong. He is saying, "Let's hold things in correct perspective." . . .
>
> Bodily exercise will help you only in this life, because when you get a new body it won't make any difference whether you've exercised this one or not.[2]

I love this reminder that all the hours we spend on our bodies will be erased the instant we are made new in heaven. They won't matter, not a minute of them. We remember this not to denounce our stewardship over the bodies we have been given but to use our minutes in them wisely! CrossFit will not enter with us into heaven, but our godliness training? That will last for eternity.

The Training Equation

Paul gives us a math equation to help us calculate how to lead our daughters well. I'm not great at math, so it's a good thing Paul keeps it simple: godliness > fitness.

Minutes in godliness training must be greater than minutes in physical training. Simple. And lest we suppose that this verse is not talking about actual minutes, Paul uses an unmistakable word: training. According to Merriam-Webster, *training* is "the act, process, or method of one that trains."[3] So we can't say, "Of course I love Jesus in my heart much more than I love exercise; therefore, godliness is way more important to me than fitness." Paul's equation does not work this way. If we make time to physically train because it is important to us, how much more should we make time to train in godliness? (Refer back to the sign in the gym quoted earlier in the chapter: "If it doesn't challenge you it won't change you.")

Our minutes do not control us; we control our minutes. We are just another part of the problem if we listen to the "experts" who say we need to be in the gym for at least thirty minutes three times a week but we don't listen to the very Word of God that tells us we need to pursue godliness first.

If I had my way, I would be in the gym every day. I love it. I love it because for some reason those minutes free my mind, and I leave that class a blank slate. But I have had to make a choice. I have only one life so I simply choose not to go every day. There are more important things I need to do. I don't mean reading my Bible and praying every single minute of every day (although I do believe that seasons of life call for this). I mean pursuing the things of God, attempting to mirror how Jesus spent his time. *That's* what I want my daughter to see. *That's* what I want her to know me for.

In our homes, as we lead our daughters toward confidence, our training time in godliness must far outweigh our training time in the gym. Our greatest fervor, our passion, and our desire for growth should direct her to the gospel. For it is the gospel alone that will not end up null and void and will not disappoint. All other training is of some value, but the value that is above all things is in our desire to grow in Christ.

Where do our daughters see that our hope lies?

If this chapter grates on you a little, you are in good company. But I believe wholeheartedly that the grating of us will help us. It will not condemn us or shame us but remind us just how important training in godliness is.

Today, let's together take fitness off the pedestal and put godliness back up there where it belongs.

That Person We Are All Thinking Of

We are not the judge of other people. We are the judge only of ourselves.

Trust me, I am with you on this one. Every time I pass by someone and hear them complaining about missing *one* of their *ten* weekly workout times, I get nauseous. Then I slap myself because I am not allowed to cast stones. If stones started flying, I'd be the first one dead. I don't get to change someone else; I only get to change me.

On the flip side, I found myself writing this chapter with a healthy concern for the women I love who are fierce about gym time but who also don't want to convey wrong messages to their daughters. I believe there is a way to be who we are naturally while still first taking aim at godliness and right perspectives of physical training.

From an Expert on Fitness

I want to introduce you to my dear friend Lauran. She attends my church and just happens to be the instructor who kicks my butt on a weekly basis at the gym. Lauran is a self-proclaimed gym rat (in fact, she introduces herself as such), and as I sat down to write this chapter, she was the first person who popped into my mind to interview. Lauran is a great example of what fitness can look like while still maintaining our faith first. And she may or may not have a T-shirt that reads, "I work out, so I can eat donuts."

Lauran is a primary certified group fitness instructor from the Athletics and Fitness Association of America, and she agreed to let me ask her some easy (and not so easy) questions. I pray that her answers help bring some balance into our homes.

Q: In your own home, how do you keep Jesus on the throne of worship over physical fitness?

A: The gym is a part of my daily routine because I love to work out. I love getting sweaty and seeing how far I can push myself. However, it is not and never has been a "gotta do" thing; rather, I *get* to do this. God gave us these cool bodies. Let's see what we can do with them! I think the gym is just like everything else—it needs to be prioritized, but it does not take precedence over God, family, or friends. Thankfully, lots of my friends are gym rats too. I do not *have* to work out every day and don't plan to be a seven-day-per-week person ever.

Q: What and how do you communicate to your children about why you love going to the gym?

A: I have a lot of energy, and so do my children. We often talk about walking/running/going to the gym as a way to get our crazy out. A good workout can make me more focused on the day. When we walk the dog in the afternoon and my youngest wants me to carry her (she's three and *very* capable of walking), I often tell her (sweetly), "No, because we all need to get our crazy out." To be honest, my kids haven't ever asked why I go to the gym so often. Perhaps because they know I work there, but more likely because that's all they've ever known. I went back to teaching classes six weeks after both of my girls were born, so they have been in child-care at the gym since they were itty-bitty. I've tried to instill in my girls that being fit looks very different on everyone. We need to stay humble in the gym just as much as we need to stay humble outside of the gym. Just because someone may be bigger than you doesn't mean they can't run circles around you.

Q: What are some of the risks you've noticed in becoming too obsessed with physical fitness?

A: The obvious—eating disorders is a big one. Another is neglecting friends and family because workouts have to get done. There was a time in my life when I almost felt guilty taking a shower if I hadn't worked out. Almost as though because I hadn't gotten sweaty I didn't deserve the shower. What?! The one and only thing we need to be "obsessed" with is loving God. Knowing him more and better so we can love others more and better. I think that sounds a bit cliché, but I kind of need to be reminded of it every Sunday because I can lean toward the obsessive side without accountability. Another obvious risk is self-righteousness because of how we look or how we feel we look. As stated earlier, we must stay humble inside and outside of the gym.

Q: How can we help our daughters develop healthy fitness habits and thoughts on weight and taking care of their bodies without damaging their confidence and then possibly putting them at risk for a poor body image?

A: Whoa. That's a tough one; these have all been tough, truth be told. I certainly think the earlier you start, the easier it may be. I didn't grow up in a house with exercise fanatics, but both of my parents were athletic. My mom was a majorette in college and my dad was in the Army for several years right out of high school. We had workout equipment at our house, but I rarely if ever saw it used. I remember getting a membership to the Y when I was in high school and we went occasionally, but we never worked out together. I did gymnastics as a little girl and then competed in high school as well as cheered. If there were ever two sports that could cause an unhealthy body image, I think those two would be it. However, my parents always told me how proud they were of me. I wasn't the best gymnast on my team by a *long* shot, but you never would've known that by the way my parents spoke about and to me. I was amazing just because I was there. They made me believe that because they believed it. I want the same for my girls. I want them to feel like they've won before they ever take the first step in a race! I just ran a 5K with my girls a few weeks ago. It was one of those tear-jerking mommy moments for me. My girls walked and ran and rode in the stroller for the entire 3.1 miles. I kept telling them how proud I was of them. They were focused on the medal they would receive after the race. I was focused on them pushing themselves and having fun, all while getting their crazy out!

We never talk about weight in our house. I've just recently gotten a scale because someone gave it to me, but it just collects dust in my bathroom. I try to focus on the things that are true about food and exercise: eating veggies is good for our bodies; if we feed our bodies good foods like fruits and veggies and meat, then our bodies will work best; if our bodies work well, we will feel great; if we feel great, we will be more motivated to be kind to our bodies by exercising. I've never been a nutrition nut, but I'm getting more and more educated as I'm entering my prime (I just turned forty). I'm not one to turn down dessert of any kind, and I think it's important that my kids see me eat healthy for the majority of the week but not deny myself (or anyone else) a treat once in a while. I love the quote "Life is short, eat dessert first." I do not eat dessert first, but I do eat dessert!

Now that's a perspective I can hold on to and teach my children with confidence: getting the crazies out *so that* I can be of sound mind in my pursuit of godliness. 'Cause, I'm just saying, there is a whole lot of crazy out there for moms and daughters alike!

Confident Mom
CHALLENGE

Challenge #6: Burn all the scales! You don't have to actually burn them; throwing them away will do just fine, but I am also a great advocate of smashing them to pieces with a sledgehammer—whatever works for you. Remove every scale from your house. If they were expensive and you need some time to adjust to a scale-less life, put them up on a closet shelf. May the absence of the scale be a statement and a claim that God and God alone gets to measure your life. No more measuring, counting, or tracking bodily successes or failures.

I suggested this challenge to a mother-daughter group once, and one mother shared with me that her daughter confessed to sneaking into her mother's room to weigh herself often. Her mother had no idea. The sweetest part of the story was how happy the daughter was at the idea of getting rid of it altogether. Amen, sister. I think it is a good idea too.

Confident Daughter
DISCUSSION QUESTIONS

1. Do you think that too many people are obsessed with "skinny"? Do you have any examples?
2. Do you have a skinny or "better" obsession that haunts you? Can you name it?
3. What are your honest perspectives on physical fitness?
4. Why do you or why don't you work out?

5. What kinds of conversations about fitness do you have in your home? How do they stack up to what God says about physical fitness in 1 Timothy 4:7–10?

6. If you could define a perfectly balanced outlook on fitness, what would you say?

7. What are some ways you can pursue godliness first?

8. Is there any view on working out in your home that you would like to alter?

9. If God has changed your heart on any of these issues, what ways can you share them with your family?

10. What do you think of the idea of getting rid of scales in your home?

11. Pray a blessing over your home. Would you pray for godliness to become the main pursuit of your family?

A Mom's Prayer

God, thank you for our bodies! Thank you that you have given us arms for carrying, legs for taking us places, and butts for sitting comfortably. You have made us just right, and we ask you now to help us treat our bodies with appreciation. We confess that we have gotten off track, that perhaps in our pursuit to be better we got lost somewhere between the physical and the spiritual. Would you bring us back? Would you give us the passion and the desire to train in godliness first? We pray that our daughters would also grow confident in this pursuit. That they would see in us a joyful change and that they would know such change came from you! God, you care about all things, and in all honesty, we pray that our daughters never give a thought to whether their arms jiggle. In Jesus's name we pray all this. Amen.

seven

Sticks and Stones

*I*t's been a rough week.

Have you ever had one like that? You know, it's right before "that" time of the month, and all of a sudden rhyme and reason go out the window.

If hormones aren't proof of the power of something unseen, I don't know what is! I have no idea what hormones look like, where they reside, or what makes them rise and fall, but I do know that they can turn a normal, halfway calm, and often reasonable Maria into a monster.

This particular week the assailant was my mind and the victim was my body. I hated all the things about all my parts, wanted to be seen in nothing but my pajamas, and hurried past the mirror on the way to the shower. I didn't want to see a thing.

And my husband, my poor husband, heard the usual questions: Honey, do you still love me the same now as you did when I was twenty? I shouldn't wear this, should I? Do these pants still look like they fit? (Gag.)

When I came out of my hormonal fog four days later, I shuddered. Who *was* that person? Ick.

We are so brutal to ourselves sometimes. We can be the most grace-filled, encouraging, and kind people on the face of the earth to others, but when it comes to ourselves we are critical, demeaning, and discouraging. I can be hard on myself and in the same breath turn to my daughter and say, "Honey, you are doing great! Don't be upset; it's okay not to be perfect!" The irony is never lost on me.

We are never going to be perfect at always loving ourselves (that is why we have Jesus, so that he can do the perfect loving). And this chapter is not about pretending that we never struggle with insecure thoughts about ourselves. We absolutely do. But I want my struggles to be mine. I want to own them and battle them with the help of God, my spouse, and my trusted friends. I do not want to make my struggles my daughter's struggles too. She has enough of her own.

If you are someone who, like me, has a history of dealing with insecurity, it is going to rear its ugly head from time to time. We will continue to fight it until we become perfect in heaven. Many times I have considered it my tiny and way whiny thorn in my side. It's okay, sisters, you are not alone, and I know that I am not either.

Raise your hand if at some point in your life you had a potty mouth. No one is watching; go ahead, you can be honest.

Okay fine, maybe not *you*, but I am sure you've known someone who has. And what happens to said potty mouth after one has children? There is an adjustment period when the parent tries to retrain their mouth. At first, the swear words still pop out, and Grandma, Aunt Sally, or your judging spouse pops you on the hand. "You want your child learning those words?!" Then maybe you try spelling them for a while. You stub your toe and out comes "C-R-A-P that hurt!" After a while, the potty mouth wanes, and you are no longer at risk of educating your child into a world of PG-13 words they don't need to learn yet.

You've succeeded. You identified the weak spot. You decided to do something about it. Then you practiced until it became natural. This is where we want to sit and chat for a little while about how to improve the way we speak about ourselves.

When we lose our confidence, we need safe places to fall apart and to run back to God so that he can help us find it over and over again. Not in us, by us, or for us but through a heavenly Father who will never let us down. When we fall (and we will fall), he is there to catch us, hold us, remind us of the truth, and then help us get back up again. In our falling and getting back up again, we can *show* our daughters how to fight. But as we stumble and fall along the way, may we leave her out of our mud. Take BFF down with us, take hubby or Mom or Grandma, but even while we sink may our arms stay strong and hold her up.

Our Words

The Bible says it, we know it, and others remind us: our words are important. Take these verses, for example: "Consider what a great forest is set on fire by a small spark. The tongue also is a fire, a world of evil among the parts of the body. It corrupts the whole body, sets the whole course of one's life on fire, and is itself set on fire by hell" (James 3:5–6).

Oh, I get it now! So that is what's happening when I am ranting and raving about who knows what at myself, my children, my husband, my friends, or my family. I've been set on fire by hell itself! It all makes sense now. I knew it felt like hell, but now we know it actually is.

I think we can already agree that this is true. We know that our words are powerful, and in many areas of our lives I believe we take great aim at taming the tongue. For example, we actively try to quit cussing, gossiping, yelling, and lying.

Amen, right? We should seek to tame these fires that come out of our mouths. But as I prayed and stewed and assessed my own words, I began to wonder if there is another brand of evil we allow to flow freely—our negative self-talk. Fellow mommas, may we identify these words and snuff them out quickly before they burn down our daughters from top to bottom.

We are our own worst critics, and entire books have been written to help us conquer the mind battles that go on inside our heads. But, in the name of Jesus, may we begin to stop these battles from coming out of our mouths, especially when we are within earshot of our girls.

"Ugh, I hate these thighs!"

"I have got to go on a diet."

"I don't look good in anything I wear."

"No, I don't want to go shopping, I hate shopping. I can never find anything that fits right."

"No cookies for me; I've gained too much weight."

"If only I was born with *her* legs."

"I look horrible today!"

"No! Don't take a picture of me. I look awful."

"I am not going out of the house; I didn't put makeup on."

Add to this list all the nicknames we have for our parts: thunder thighs, bubble butt, jiggle arms, belly pooch, frumpy, lanky, and so on.

I know, sister, I'm living there with you too. Feels kind of gross to read on paper, right? But I pray that guilt would flee far from us. Guilt is the enemy's scheme when growth is God's desire.

I was sharing these thoughts with a dear friend of mine and she said, "I know! My daughter even noticed the look I gave myself when I looked in the mirror, and I wasn't even trying to give myself a look!" We want our girls to listen to us, and we forget they watch and learn from us 24/7. We want our girls to learn how they should talk about themselves from us.

It's like accents. In the Furlough home, we do not say the word *fat*, we do not make fun of one another's bodies, and we say "you guys" instead of "y'all." I grew up in Connecticut. I could not say *y'all* right even if I tried. I am a northerner; I speak Yankee. Even though all my children were born and bred in North Carolina, they speak Yankee too.

Why is that when they are surrounded by y'alls? How is it that my children can't say *y'all* right either? They can't speak Southern because they talk like my husband and me. We learn how to speak from our parents. We learn our native tongue from the house we are raised in.

What is your native tongue? Do your words reflect your heavenly Father? Do your words uphold your body like the beautiful gift from God that it is, or do you constantly put yourself down? Do you talk about your body as if it is for *using* and *being* and *doing*, or do you talk about your body like it is for *looking at* or *growing* or *shrinking*? Are clothes your enemy, or are they a blessing? Are your words fiery flames that burn you, or are they encouraging reflections of the way God himself sees you?

I know that I won't be able to protect my daughter from all destructive words. We parents pray and hope that our children are not ridiculed or made fun of in school, and we go to great lengths to prevent it. We are ready and armed for what to say and do when it does happen. But I don't want to be so distracted by the potential words of others that I forget about the power of my own. In the name of Jesus, I pray we learn to protect our daughters from our words.

Words of Confidence

Speaking with confidence gets a bad rap. When confident words flow through our minds, they sound prideful, and so we dismiss them. I think all we really need is a tiny little perspective shift.

If our words are meant merely to make us feel better or if we put others down to build ourselves up, we have a problem with pride.

But if our confident words glorify God and lift up our daughters, then we need to get talking! I propose that when we speak sweetly of ourselves, we do both.

Imagine that you are walking through God's living room. Jesus is lovingly giving you a tour of his home. He points to a painting and says, "My Father made this." He points to a sculpture and says again, "This was made by my Father." Now imagine that in response you say, "That is awful! It's not shaped correctly, the colors are way off, and I really don't like the shading. What was he thinking when he made that?"

I picture Jesus weeping. I imagine Jesus wishing that instead we would view and trust God as being a perfect imaginer.

Let's rewind the story and practice responding differently. "Wow," we say, "what an honor to behold the work of God. It does not look like anything I could make. How mysterious are his ways, and I admire his work even though I cannot fully understand it!" See the difference? We don't always need to fully comprehend something to praise it.

Now let's go to a different home—our home. Standing in front of a mirror, we berate what we see. We yell, we cry, we condemn, and we nitpick because the reflection we see never matches up to our vision of perfect. We are not kind with our words; we put ourselves down and down and down until we are so low that we can never imagine getting up again. Our words have done that.

As we look up, we see something that shocks us. We see two extra feet. Our daughter is there, in the mirror, and through our own reflection she waits. She is, after all, created from us. She is a part of us, she is a reflection of us, she even has some of our parts. If we hate *our* bodies, how can we teach her to love *hers*? We are so closely linked.

So, we rise, we stand up with a new mission, and this time when we look into the mirror we allow ourselves to see her face too. We don't fully have the words yet, so we mutter God's words instead. We look in the mirror and, based on Psalm 139, we sing praises to ourselves.

I am created perfectly.

I am God's masterpiece.

All of my parts were put in place by a God who loves me.

I am wonderfully made.

I am made with a purpose and for a purpose.

All of my days, all of me, and everything that holds me together is God's.

God's thoughts are precious; therefore, when he thinks of me he is in awe of me—therefore, I am in awe of me!

It's not about me. I can say these things with bold confidence because deep down I know they are not for me at all. They are for God, and they are for my daughter, and I don't care who hears or judges me. I will stand tall in front of that mirror and practice praising what I see until one day I begin to believe it.

It's okay, sisters. We can feel comfortable saying it even before we truly believe it. I believe the sincerity comes after the practice (it did for me). So we train our tongues and keep reign over them even when the hormonal monsoons hit or the jeans are a little tight.

I will keep trying if you will.

When Our Daughters Say, "I'm Fat"

"Mom, I am so fat." What is a mother to say? Or what about this one: "Mom, I think *she* is fat."

We cannot leave a chapter about words without brainstorming this issue together. We all have heard it, it always breaks our hearts, and 100 percent of the time it's not true. I don't care who you are, I don't care what size or shape you are, the word *fat* (and all the negative connotations that come with it) is plain and simple not an appropriate description for any one of God's creation. Especially not our daughters who, just yesterday, were playing My Little Pony in the middle of the hallway. It just can't be. We have to do something. We have to change something. But before we do any of that, we have to try not to freak out!

A few weeks ago, we held a leadership training at our church for women who feel called and passionate about leading. One session in particular, taught by my friend Lillie, stood out to me. Before having kiddos, Lillie worked for Dr. Henry Cloud, and for the last decade, she has coached executives for a leadership development company. Her session was on reflective listening, based on a curriculum written by Christina Kisley.

I have always thought I was a good listener, but a quote she shared from Dr. Cloud's book *Integrity* stopped me dead in my tracks.

> We have all seen those instances where someone (maybe even ourselves) has said something negative like "I'm such a loser," and someone immediately comes back with "Don't say that! You don't really feel that way!" or some other attempt to help that only drives the person further into hopelessness. The reason is that he now has two problems. He has the initial problem that he felt so negative about, and then he feels that he is all alone and has no one who truly understands. That is why people who try to help others by talking them out of what they feel are usually no help at all. It is also the reason why research has for decades proven that you can help desperate people immensely by giving them no answers at all, and only giving them empathy.[1]

In wanting to save my daughter, could I really be making things worse for her?

It is a painful truth that we cannot use our words to convince our daughters out of their own negative self-talk. We have but two weapons up our sleeves: our *example* and our *empathy*.

Since learning about reflective listening a few weeks ago, I have been practicing on my kids. Here is the short version of how it works that my brain retained from the session: do *not* ask *any* questions or make *any* statements until you have restated what your child has said back to them in such a way that they finally give you a yes.

Let me tell you, this is hard. But it has been paying high dividends. My kiddos have been going deeper into conversations. When a child says something to us, and we come back with a statement or question of our own, we are taking control of the situation, but with reflective listening, they get to lead the discussion where they want it to go. Shall we practice?

First, let's look at a conversation without reflective listening.

Daughter: "Mom, I am so fat!"

Mom: "Honey, no! You are *not* fat. You are beautiful just the way you are."

Daughter: "You have to say that to me, you are my mom."

Mom: "That's not true! Well, I mean, it is true, I am your mom. But I promise I am not just saying that. I really believe it."

Daughter: "Whatever, Mom."

End of conversation. Somehow, even with our best intentions, we ended up making the conversation about us. What started as a cry for understanding ended up in a court of law–type discussion with us trying to convince our daughter (jury) that we do have the ability to be objective.

Now let's try it using reflective listening.

Daughter: "Mom, I am so fat!"

Mom: "What I hear you saying is that you think you are fat."

Daughter: "Well, I mean, I know I'm not really fat, but a lot of times I just feel like I am."

Mom: "Sometimes you feel like you are fat."

Daughter: "I mean, well, Suzy in my math class is just so much tinier than me, and when I look at her it makes me think that I must be fat."

Mom: "I understand, honey. What I hear you saying is that when you look at Suzy, you then think that you might be fat."

Daughter: "Yeah, Mom."

Now we have something! By simply restating the same statements she was making to us, we were able to do three things:

1. Take a deep breath to get our brains and prayers together as to the best way to respond.
2. Go three levels deeper to discern the real reason she was saying she is fat.
3. Offer her empathy and understanding instead of trying to prove her feelings wrong.

This one simple change in our conversations can prove so powerful. I confess that after I started practicing this with my children, I began to experience some unexpected sadness. As I was listening to them, truly listening to them, little Maria began to pop up into my mind. She never felt heard or understood. She always thought there was something wrong with her, and any time she tried to share, she just always felt like her feelings were wrong.

But, after all, how can feelings be wrong? We feel what we feel, yes? Little Maria just needed to be listened to. She needed some empathy and a hug that said, "This is hard; let's talk about it some more."

Friends, my mom was in that reflective listening session with me, and afterward (with tender tears) we got the chance to talk about it. I'm not sure whom I felt worse for—little Maria or my mom. She just hadn't known about all this. There was no road map through her own struggles and emotions nor any books or training on how to help me handle mine. She didn't know what she didn't know, and I hold no blame against her whatsoever. But, sisters, we now know.

We know! We have now been given the blessing (and the curse) of knowledge. I say blessing and curse because this is not easy. You know when these reflective listening times are going to come? One split second after my daughter mouths off to me about not having the right snacks in the pantry for school. Or after the forty-five-hundredth time I said that it is time for bed! Or right in the middle of my own bloated PMS-ing struggle of a week.

These times for listening and empathy sound so lovely and put together on the page, but in real life they are messy and hard. Trust me, that first time I had to go an entire five sentences without asking a question just about killed me! My whole body almost burst trying to hold in all my comments and analyses. Email me and let me know what it was like for you. We can laugh, cry, and complain together so that we can put our game faces on when we are with our children.

And may the God who has the power to raise from death to life remind us each day that his Holy Spirit in us is our biggest hope for setting the example and offering the empathy.

From an Expert on Words

My friend and fellow Revell author Meredith McDaniel is an amazing counselor to young women. She has a huge heart for teens, and she and her husband serve faithfully in Young Life. Meredith and I often have conversations about confidence and the importance of the role of moms in our daughters' lives. I picked her brain about the value of positive self-talk.

Q: Meredith, from your counseling perspective, what are some of the main reasons why we should be intentional about the words we use around our daughters?

A: Young women pick up on even our most subtle cues and words. When our daughters see, hear, and perceive our subtlety, seeds are planted in them. The seeds planted in kids' minds can either haunt or help them for a lifetime. I think this is something we all have personal stories about, times when we were young that we can remember exactly what someone said about our bodies or our weight or something we were eating that stuck with us into adulthood.

Just recently, I have been thinking back to a time when I was young. I was standing by a piano with one of my best friends, and we were practicing a solo for a song at church. The words my piano teacher spoke to my friend stuck with me as seeds as they seemed to imply that my friend was better than me and that I shouldn't ever sing in front of anyone ever again because I wasn't good enough. I am in my midthirties and I am still processing those words! Something so small can stick and fester for years.

Q: Oh, my goodness, yes! I think we all can relate to that with a story of our own. Can you explain a little more about what happens in a young woman's brain when she watches her mom look in the mirror or hears her commenting about herself?

A: Our words and actions are very powerful, and young women are so much more observant than we realize. They are looking for us to be an example even when they would never say that to us. This is so important for us to understand, because words we hear and experiences we have when we are young become permanent pathways in our brain.

For example, when a young woman sees her mom get on the scale and make a funny face or hears her say something negative when she looks in the mirror, she is watching and interpreting what her mom is doing. Even our smallest words or facial expressions can be completely misinterpreted because of what is going on in their brains neurologically. Developmentally, in teens the amygdala in the back of their brain develops sooner than the frontal cortex. The amygdala runs on emotion and the frontal cortex runs on logic, and because of that teenagers run with their emotions during an event rather than considering logically what actually happened. The pathways (or memories) are formed in their brain based on the emotions or feelings they had more than the actual information. They cannot yet use logic from their frontal cortex to rationalize and think through the facts. They cannot say to themselves, *Just because my mom says that about herself does not mean it is true about me* or *Just because I am feeling this way does not make it true*. They are developmentally not able to comprehend logic over emotions just yet.

Q: Thank you, Meredith! You have officially explained to me my entire adolescence. How my poor mom talked about her thighs was seared into my brain, and because I was a self-focused and emotionally processing teenager, I implanted into my brain as fact, "I am going to have fat thighs and I am going to hate them." Makes so much sense now. Do you have any encouragement for moms?

A: The best encouragement I can give to moms is that we have a high honor and opportunity to be a unique, life-giving voice to our daughters and other young women in our lives. First and foremost, we must take the time to find our own worth and identity in our Maker before we can expect our daughters to do the same. For me this looks like saying positive things about myself, both internally and out loud around my family. I also take intentional opportunities to do the same for my daughter, and I can see how it deeply affects her spirit every time! Eventually, this language will translate into a dialogue in both of our minds that will follow us around for life and give us the confidence we need to thrive. That being said, if you do or say something that in retrospect you realize may have been harmful to your daughter, address it with her! Tell her how it made you feel, and ask her how it made her feel. Clear communication is better than leaving things unsaid, and grace covers it all.

Confident Mom
CHALLENGE

Challenge #7: Make a list titled "10 Things I Love about Me" and share it with your daughter. Try to include some body parts. While your entire list doesn't need to be physical attributes, I think it is helpful for our daughters to hear that it is good to love our parts and pieces. It might be tough but take some time to sit with her and share your list. What you say to her may sound something like this: "Honey, I am not sure if I spend enough time saying positive things about myself. I am going to try to be better about that, and to help get started, would you mind if I share with you this list I made?" Or perhaps write it down and slip it to her in her room or post it on the refrigerator.

Bonus Challenge: If the conversation goes well and your daughter receives your list with an open mind, ask her if she would be willing to make a "10 Things I Love about Me" list too, and ask if she would share it with you.

Confident Daughter
DISCUSSION QUESTIONS

1. Give an example of a time you overheard someone saying something negative about themselves when they didn't know you were listening.

2. Can you share about a time that someone said something negative to you or around you that stuck with you for a really long time?

3. Daughter, what kinds of words do you hear your mom say about herself?

4. Mom, what kinds of words do you hear your daughter say about herself?

5. What are some words, sayings, or comments that, from here on out, you want to ban from your home?

6. Proverbs 31:25–26 says, "She is clothed with strength and dignity; she can laugh at the days to come. She speaks with wisdom, and faithful instruction is on her tongue." What are some ways we can work words of laughter, wisdom, and God's truth into our conversations?

7. Are there any lies you believe about your body that today, here and now, you want to replace with truth? State the lie and then name the truth.

8. Come up with a catchphrase or a funny one-liner you can use to call each other out when you are using negative words about yourself.

A Mom's Prayer

Father God, our inner critic is so very loud. The lies we believe about ourselves are so convincing that it is hard to silence them sometimes. Because we love your creation and desire to protect our daughters, would you help us to tame our tongues? Would you help us become more aware of the words we are using, and would you give us self-control to keep our mouths shut when we are tempted to be self-critical? God, we know that you love us, but we have an enemy that whispers constantly in our ears that we are not good enough, we are ugly, we need improving. By the power that is given to us through the Holy Spirit and through Christ's death for us, would you help us fend off those whispers? They are not true, and they wreak havoc on our hearts. In the meantime, Lord, while you work on our strength, help us to practice using only your words. Protect our girls from our tongues, and make our homes places filled with confidence from words and conversations that build up. It's in Jesus's name we pray. Amen!

eight

On the Cover of a Magazine

I'll never forget the very first time I looked in the mirror and thought I was fat. I was nine years old and spending my Saturday afternoon as I always did—locked in my room with a teen *Bop* magazine.

The afternoon festivities went something like this. First, I went to extreme lengths to make sure neither my parents nor my younger brother entered my room without first alerting me. Second, I needed a soundtrack, which usually included Wilson Phillips or New Kids on the Block. But most important was the full-length mirror.

That full-length mirror entertained me for hours. I would pose, dance, sing, model, dress up, imitate my parents, and put on makeup all in front of that full-length reflection. But this Saturday, this specific Saturday, would forever change the way I looked into that mirror.

I was reading *Bop*, and, truth be told, the pictures were the only thing that really mattered. I would go through the pages, find a picture of a girl I thought was cool, and then pose like her in the mirror. On this Saturday, a picture of Tiffani Amber Thiessen stood out to me. She was propped up against a locker with one leg up and her hands on her hips. Now it was my turn. I carefully propped up against my dresser in order to copy her perfectly. I put one leg up and hands on my hips. I remember the feelings of dread and sadness that came over me as I looked in the same full-length mirror that had previously brought me innocent views of myself. My next thoughts were, to this day, embedded permanently in my mind: *I don't look like her; I am not as skinny as she is.* And that was it. From then on, the comparison game began. The realization hit me like a ton of bricks: I don't look like those girls in the magazines.

Today, images of women just like Tiffani Amber Thiessen are plastered everywhere (no longer in magazines only and now wearing a lot less than overalls and a tank top). Also, the content that was available to me only in the form of a magazine now comes streaming into our lives everywhere. I don't need to go to great lengths to describe the magnitude of the social media problem that exists today. We live knee deep in it, and all the experts from sea to shining sea are yelling out with one voice: we need to be careful and we need to guard our children! Social media feeds + prone to insecurity and poor body image = bad.

But what can we do? Better yet, what would God have us do?

Before we begin, let's make an agreement. Let's not use this time to judge, compare, or feel guilty about our home's policy on media. I have sat in enough of these discussions with moms to know it never ends well. One mom doesn't allow anything that powers on in her home, another mom has a five-year-old with a Facebook account, and we are left with a piled-high mass of insecure moms. Myself included.

We all need rules, and we all need boundaries. But for us, for now, media rules aside, let's get started.

Why I Can't

I was in my dorm room, sophomore year in college, and I couldn't get out of bed.

Somewhere around senior year in high school I found diet pills. *Lose Weight Fast! Suppress Your Appetite and Watch the Pounds Fall! Control Your Size Today!* Wow, really? Can it be that easy? Apparently, it can, and all it took was $17.99 at the grocery store a couple times per month.

And it worked. The pounds started falling off and the compliments started raging: "Wow, Maria, you look amazing!" "Maria, you are making the rest of us look bad!" "Look at you in that bathing suit; you go, girl!"

I'm not sure whether it was the diet pills or the attention, but something about the whole thing became addicting and I felt like I couldn't live without them. But like every addiction, you always need more. By sophomore year I needed the "stronger" diet pills, the ones you could only get on the internet.

Finally, my body said, "No more," and I was sick and stuck in bed. It was also around this time that I began to learn about Jesus. I saw my family back home enter into this new relationship, this new faith, and God began to stir in me. *Maria, get up and get help.* Thankfully, most colleges offer free counseling, and I went.

The advice my counselor shared with me was life altering. It still affects me to this day, and I filter much of my social media choices through his words: "Maria, what I want you to do is go home on Thanksgiving break and communicate to your family that you need for them to stop making any comments about the way you look, good or bad. Negative comments about your body affect you poorly, but so do positive comments. All of their words feed into the lie that your body and your looks are what matter most and that if you don't look a certain way you are a failure." These words were a soothing balm to my soul.

This conversation with my family was one of the hardest I've ever had. Not only did I need the courage to share my struggles with them, but I also had to muster up the guts to ask them to stop doing something. I had to ask them to give me words that 100 percent of the time focused on who I was and not how I looked.

When I am on social media, I become that teenage girl all over again. The words coming at me now span far beyond the people I see most often in person. Now words come at me from unlimited directions. Online presences thrust me back into the world of comparing and contrasting, making sure I smooth over the bags under my eyes, and only posting from that angle I think flatters me most. It's too much for me; I am not good at coping with it. So for the protection of my own soul and spirit, I can't go there very often.

I've been ashamed of this truth for many years. I am not very popular when I'm completely unaware of the birth of so and so's sweet baby, I am never on top of birthdays, and surely I am the black sheep of the family who never comments. Then I became a writer, and Satan started in: "You want to succeed as an author, don't you? Well then, you must be on social media more. Way more."

I bit into that apple again. For a time, I thought I could do it, but the truth that God had already taught me came quickly and utterly back into play: your confidence can't handle it, and this does not make you a failure.

So here is my list of reasons why this insecuraholic has to limit social media:

It's visual, and it tempts me to focus on the physical.

Seeing scantily clothed bodies always makes me feel worse about myself.

The "likes" and the compliments make things worse—they are never enough and have addicting qualities.

The attention is bad for my God-centered confidence and lures me toward man-centered confidence.

It tricks me into believing that mass truth is God's truth.

This is *my* truth. This is *my* story and it heavily impacts how I lead my children. I ask you: What is your truth? What is your social media story? How does it impact how you lead your daughter?

We have to figure this out for ourselves before we can know which direction to lead her in.

It is messy. We live in such a visual world that it is nearly impossible to pull our daughters fully out of it. Our best chance is to learn how to navigate it ourselves so that we can offer them direction and the solutions that have worked for us.

Truth Be Told

We are going to take a deep dive. Even as I write this, I pray you will come with me and that you trust we will together end up in a place that makes full sense and has everything to do with our security. Following are three ways to guard our hearts when using social media. For even with all that social media offers, the truth of God's Word is really all we have.

Colossians 2:6–7

So then, just as you received Christ Jesus as Lord, continue to live your lives in him, rooted and built up in him, strengthened in the faith as you were taught, and overflowing with thankfulness.

In all the circumstances we face, even on social media, may we remember to stake claim to the fact that when we receive Christ as Lord we are "rooted and built up in him." Our daughters too. We can wander into these places with her, because ultimately we trust that she is Jesus's even more than she is ours. May we remember our faith is like a tree with deep, strong roots. As we wander deep into the vast forest of the media world, may we keep our eyes focused on our deeply rooted faith in Christ and cling to God and God alone.

Mother and Daughter Media Heart Guard #1: Every time we enter into the media world, say a brief prayer: "Lord, keep me rooted in you."

Colossians 2:8

See to it that no one takes you captive through hollow and deceptive philosophy, which depends on human tradition and the elemental spiritual forces of this world rather than on Christ.

Many messages are close to the truth. Especially when people use the term *Christian* on their profile, we turn our sensors down and think we can believe everything they say or post. We have become far too trusting, and it makes me angry with a fiery righteous anger when I see people flaunting their half-biblical, hollow, and deceptive philosophies. I never want you to listen to just me. I pray that you see God through me, but at the end of every word, picture, blog post, and book, the one thing that really matters is God's truth.

Our current human tradition is what our daughters are growing up in, with the basic principles of this world assuring them there is no ultimate truth. It takes regular exposure to God's Word to be able to discern the lies from the truth. I pray, sweet momma, that you will join me in making sure that a welcomed part of our days is even a small session of Bible reading. I understand that this intimidates many. I have heard and experienced "I can't understand it at all" or "It's so hard to read" or "I don't like some of the things I learn about God." Sisters, we have to keep trying. If we don't hold God's truth in our hearts, then how do we know truth when we hear it?

> Mother and Daughter Media Heart Guard #2: Pick a social media or blog post and practice identifying the "hollow and deceptive" philosophies that are based on human tradition.

Colossians 2:9–10

For in Christ all the fullness of the Deity lives in bodily form, and in Christ you have been brought to fullness. He is the head over every power and authority.

With Christ in us, we are the boss. We answer to *no one* before him. Not our BFF, not our mother-in-law, not our peers, not our children. Christ is the only one given full authority over us. Do we need to have mutual respect and kindness for all these important people in our lives? Absolutely! But when our heads hit the pillow at night, we don't have to be concerned about pleasing anyone other than Jesus.

When I am tempted to feel guilty because I did not do that online thing "everyone else is doing," I have to remind myself that I've been given the authority to make any choice I determine will be pleasing to Christ rather than people. And if my choice is to guard my insecure heart and not give into something I am not entirely sure aligns with what the Bible says, I am good with that. I must remind myself and practice being okay with that.

> Mother and Daughter Media Heart Guard #3: In every online choice we make, we ask ourselves, *Am I making this choice to please man or to please God?*

These principles may not be world changers, but I pray that as we use social media, they might just act as little nudges to spur us on *toward* God instead of *away from* God. Listen, I realize we cannot fully change the environment in which our children are growing up. I am also not the mom who is going to always take all the things away. But I think it's wise to arm ourselves with tools when we watch something, post something, or "like" something. While we cannot make our daughters use the tools we offer them, it shouldn't stop us from trying.

When they see us, when they watch what we watch and see what we see, may they observe someone who does not take things lightly or lying down. My children often see and hear me wrestling through decisions about what I watch or what social media I participate in.

One evening I was having a conversation with my daughter and lovingly prepping her for the fact that she would not be getting a phone until she was a certain age. Together we talked about the pros and cons of that decision and why it was not an easy choice. I was praying under my breath with every sentence, and I said to her, "Honey, I am not going to lie to you; many times having a phone feels like a heavy burden to me. I spend so much emotional and mental energy trying to figure out what to do and what not to do, and that is not a burden I want you to have to carry yet. Be free as long as you can!"

Her response to me was so sweet I wanted to capture it in a locket and keep it around my neck for safekeeping. She said, "I know, Mom. I guess it's not going to bother me that I don't have one; it's just going to be so annoying that everyone else will be on theirs all the time." I know, right?!

I had to pinch myself. I stumbled into a conversation about social media with a preteen that somehow went well! After I looked out the window to make sure pigs were not flying or Jesus wasn't coming back, I took mental notes of the circumstances surrounding our conversation. Here are the observations I made about my discussion with her:

- It was at a low-stress moment.
- We were both in good moods going into it.
- It was unplanned.
- I had no agenda.
- I gave her the freedom to disagree with me.
- I didn't downplay the importance that social media and cell phones can have. (Even though personally and deep down I sometimes hate them and wish I could just go eat locusts in the desert with John the Baptist, I realize not everyone shares my sentiments.)

As we explore our own heart, motivations, and media choices, I pray that we grab our girls and take them along on the journey with us. It is for certain that none of us have it all figured out, and we could use some traveling companions as we seek God's best for how we encounter social media.

From a Facebook Expert

Kristen Hatton is the author of *The Gospel-Centered Life in Exodus for Students*, *Face Time: Your Identity in a Selfie World*, and *Get Your Story Straight: A Teen's Guide to Learning and Living the Gospel*. She has a passion and love for teaching youth God's truth and has dug deep into the struggles that being in a social media world can cause us. It is my honor and pleasure to share her thoughts with you.

Q: In your research and experience, how does our media consumption affect our own insecurity and body image?

A: For both women and teens, research shows a direct correlation between high media use and body image issues. The greater our exposure to images of beautiful, fit, and/or thin women, the more likely we are to compare ourselves with others and grow discontent with our own bodies. This is especially true for women and girls who already feel insecure about their bodies.

In my own research and ministry, I have realized that even those women or girls who look like they have it all are not immune to self-scrutiny and comparisons. But we all tend to think we are the only ones who struggle in this way. Instead of talking about it to realize we are all in the same boat, we become increasingly down on ourselves and jealous of others. In large part, I believe this is the cause of the increase in mental health issues—such as anxiety, depression, and eating disorders—that we are seeing.

Q: How do pictures affect our self-perception?

A: It is easy to look at social media and assume all our friends have the "perfect" life. Most often, what we are seeing is their best foot forward and their best days. The irony is that we post our own versions of our best self with similar scenarios, though we know the truths behind the facade. We know if our pictures have been carefully edited to camouflage the wrinkles or the extra pounds and that the cute outfit we have on is not our norm. But even so, when we see others looking beautiful, doing something fun, or gathering with other people, we often start to compare their "best self" to our regular day. And all of a sudden we can feel lonely, less than, or depressed.

Q: If we struggle with insecurity, what are some ways to guard ourselves when we use social media?

A: Depending on the intensity of the struggle, it may be wise to delete social media, even if just temporarily. This is something my daughter did for a time until she felt like she could be on Instagram without comparing herself to others.

If we are on social media and find that we begin spiraling downward in our thinking about ourselves, this is a good indication it is time to close it and ask God to protect us from the lies and to rest in his truth.

We should also take note of what those triggers are that lead us toward comparison and feeling less than. Is it a certain person's posts or a certain type of posts? Maybe following lifestyle bloggers or fitness inspiration posts isn't right for you? Maybe you need to unfollow someone?

Another practical tip would be to set a time limit to your social media scrolling or set only a certain time per day that you get on. There is a great app called Moments that monitors the amount of time you spend on your phone. This can provide a great wake-up call, and you can even set it so that an alarm goes off after you've reached the allotted time you've allowed for yourself.

But most importantly, we need to ask God for his protection and his grace to keep our minds set on his Word. We need to be in his Word so that we have his truth to counter the lies that crop up in our minds.

Q: What does God-centered confidence look like on social media?

A: God-centered confidence on social media looks like cheering others on as opposed to feeling threatened by what you see. It's the ability to feel genuine delight over someone else's experiences, beauty, and happiness, knowing it doesn't diminish anything about you. In this sense, it is a modern working out of loving your neighbor as yourself. But the only way we can have this kind of God-centered confidence is to know that our identity is securely rooted in him. This takes a constant reorienting of our minds off the lies and onto the truth about who he is and who we are in him.

Confident Mom
CHALLENGE

Challenge #8: Go on a total media fast (I recommend a week, but you do you). No social media, no TV, no magazines, no news, no Netflix, and so on. Don't be scared! I know it sounds intimidating, but doing this will teach you so much about yourself. When I went on my media fast, God gave me great clarity on many of my fears and insecurities. It turns out that for me, much of my media consumption only enhanced some of the issues I already had. Media did not cause my fear or insecurity, but it did throw gasoline on those fires. After my media fast, I chose to add only half of them back into my life. I cut many out entirely and have never looked back!

Bonus Challenge: Do a whole-house media fast! Crawl in a hole and die, right? Because your family will hate you? I hear you. It's a brave call, but I do believe everyone *might* survive. Maybe try your media fast first, and then (because you loved it so much) share with your family the impact it had on you and implement one as a family. It might work best to offer up to the group the decision about how long the fast will be. Have a good ol' bartering session in which everyone participates, even dads. You guys got this! I know you do.

Confident Daughter
DISCUSSION QUESTIONS

1. Have you ever seen a picture or a video of another woman that made you feel bad about yourself? Tell the story.

2. When you are browsing through your news feed, how does it usually make you feel?

3. How does it feel when you post something that gets a lot of positive comments?

4. How does it feel when you post something and no one responds or you get negative comments?

5. Do you think our relationship with God can help us when we are on social media or watching something? How?

6. Do you think God cares about what we watch or what we say or do on social media? Why or why not?

7. What is a quick prayer we can say before each time we go on social media?

8. What are some "hollow and deceptive" philosophies we come in contact with online?

9. Why do you think we often have the desire to please other people before we please God?

10. Do you have any boundaries over media in your life? What are they and why do you have them?

11. What do you think about this Bible verse: "Do not be misled: 'Bad company corrupts good character'" (1 Cor. 15:33)?

A Mom's Prayer

Father, you are the God of all things. We ask that you help us to remember that you are master over everything in this world, even our social media news feeds. Would you help us to seek you first in all of these things and help us to discern what is harmful for us? God, our daughters need you to be a loud and clear voice when so many other voices seem louder. We give them over to you and ask that you would protect them and intercede on their behalf when words and pictures meet their eyes. We pray that your still and small voice would be more powerful than all the others. God, give us and our daughters wisdom far beyond our understanding. Give us self-control beyond what we are capable of and help us know what media battles are worth fighting. Forgive us now for any ways we have previously left you out of this area of our lives, and give us new hope as we welcome you in with open arms! Amen.

nine

Helping Her *Love* How She Looks

A narrative written by my daughter, Faith Furlough.

Daughter:

As I slowly opened my eyes, I could see only bits of light. When my eyes fully opened, I turned my head slightly so I could see the window. There were early morning rays seeping through, and I slowly lifted my tired body. My mom and I had things to do early in the day, so I finally got up and made my bed.

I put on my favorite dress and shoes, but before I left I found myself taking a look around my room. My artwork on the wall, my stuffed animals on the bed, and then a Bible verse caught my eye. Proverbs 31:25: "She is clothed with strength and dignity." I read it, left the room, and closed the door.

When I got into my bathroom, I looked in the mirror and thought, *I am beautiful*. When I walked down the hall, I saw Mom walking toward me.

Mom:

Right as I opened my eyes, I thought about what I was going to do that day. A smile spread across my face as I thought about it. I loved going to do things with my daughter.

I hopped right out of bed and hoped my daughter was already awake. I put my favorite dress on; it was the one that matched my daughter's, along with the shoes. When I got into the bathroom, I was thinking about putting my hair up, then my eye caught the Bible verse on my mirror. Proverbs 31:25: "She is clothed with strength and dignity." Then I remembered, I was perfect just the way I was. I thought, *I am beautiful.*

I walked into the hallway and saw my daughter walking toward me.

The mom and the daughter smiled when they saw each other. They were on their way to teach other girls and women about being confident in who God made them.

The Confidence Story

Faith has no interest in writing that nonfiction mumbo jumbo. She is a fiction writer all the way. So when I asked her if she wanted to share anything in this book she said, "Well, can I write a fiction short story?"

I gave her the topic, prayed for God to give her the words, and sent her on her way. This beautiful piece is what she returned with. I was astonished at how she captured confidence so perfectly.

On the surface, this chapter can seem to undo everything we have talked about thus far. Why do we need to love how we look? Isn't our true beauty in our godly character? Looks are not what really matter, right? The reason we need to love how we look is because freedom comes when we do. There is no good whatsoever that comes with hating the way we look and being so self-critical that all we ever see in ourselves is bad. No, beauty is not about outward appearance; yes, God has made us for a greater purpose; and yes, spending too much attention on our looks causes more harm than good. But we don't have to deny any of these truths in order to get practical.

So let's get our hands dirty together, figure out tangible ways that can help us love the way we look, and then help our daughters to love the way they look as well. Before we begin, I'd like to say two things:

1. The following strategies have worked for me. If you had pulled me aside fifteen years ago and whispered, "Someday you will love how you look," I would have laughed, hard. But when the bad feelings come and the negativity comes, I grab on to one of these and it helps. I pray they may help you and your daughter too.

2. This section is for you to communicate directly to your daughter! Take one at a time (you don't need to throw them at her all at once), but teach her the ones you think will help her. While the rest of the book has been for you to model, this chapter is for you to teach.

To learn to love how we look (gulp), let's consider the following ideas. May Jesus be our guide!

Say It First, Believe It Second

We spent an entire chapter on true beauty; by this point I pray that Proverbs 31 is implanted in your heart and mind for always. God's truth is in that passage, and Hebrews 4:12 says, "For the word of God is alive and active. Sharper than any double-edged sword, it penetrates even to dividing soul and spirit, joints and marrow; it judges the thoughts and attitudes of the heart." I pray that the verses you have read in this book multiply to create great dividends in you and your home.

So how about we let the truth of God do its work in us, and (while we wait) we just start? We know that our true beauty comes from things unseen, the ways God has left his fingerprint on us. But we must also have the courage to acknowledge our outward beauty. It's okay to think we are beautiful. It is even okay to say it; in fact, it's more than okay. It is important that we say it *out loud*!

I think too often we wait to start saying something about ourselves until we believe it, but why wait? To love how you look, start saying you do (even if you don't believe it yet). Say it in the mirror when you wake up in the morning; say it before you go to bed at night; say it to your daughter: "Why yes, honey, I *do* love how I look!" Say it in different tones and different pitches:

I am beautiful. (high voice)
I am beautiful. (low voice)
I love how I look. (robot voice)
I love my body. (helium voice)
I love myself, inside and out. (New York accent)
Y'all, I am beautiful just the way I am. (Southern belle)

Just keep saying it. Just keep swimming, swimming, swimming, *swimming*. What am I doing? Swimming!

I am beautiful, beautiful, beautiful, *beautiful*. What am I? Beautiful!

Have I been repetitive enough about the repetition yet?

Encourage your daughter to say it about herself too. Have a completely awkward date and say it out loud to one another: "I am beautiful." See who can go the longest without laughing.

Now, I am not a proponent of lying. In fact, since Jesus asks us not to, I am quite stringent on my "no lying" life policy, and my kids know that lying is an offense of epic proportions. So even on the days when I don't really mean the "I am beautiful" statement, let's not consider it a lie as much as a proclamation of a promise of what is to come.

There is power in telling yourself you are beautiful, and (though it might sound embarrassing at first) we have got to do the silly and awkward thing of teaching our daughters to practice loving themselves with their audible words.

Come on, one more time just for me. Before we move on to the next section, say it with me: "I am beautiful." Who cares if you are in a public place? Whisper it under your breath! It is great practice for that überfun conversation you are about to have with your daughter when you tell her you have been doing this yourself.

Wear Clothes That Make You Feel Beautiful

Remember the story I shared earlier in the book about ripping the jeans off my body? Well, that almost happened again.

Call it expansion from the heat, call it a few extra pounds, call it bloating—don't know, don't care. All I know is that one particular morning my jeans were not having it. They were tight and uncomfortable, and my mind flashed back to thirteen-year-old me in my room. I started sweating, and the voices in my head began battling.

First, the lies say to me, "Look at you, you are a failure. Those jeans don't fit you because you failed and gained weight."

Then truth whispers, "You know full well that these jeans are not a reflection of your worth."

Lies say, "Rip them off. Do it, just like you did when you were a girl. You haven't changed a bit, you know."

Truth says, "You have been made new; you are a new creation. The old self has passed away."

Lies say, "Rip them off and then lose weight."

Truth says, "Take them off, spend some time with the Lord sharing how you feel, and then move along. Don't believe the lies."

Deep breath. Victory bell goes to truth.

I took the jeans off and threw them away. I don't need jeans to have power over me! I don't need them in my closet as a physical reminder of what I am not. I always hated those jeans anyway; they only ever made me feel less than. The only reason I kept them around was to torture myself, like some sort of self-demeaning motivation. I treated those jeans as if their existence would make me strive harder.

Done with that! Can we be done with that? Can we teach our girls to be done with that too? No more clothes that don't make us feel (a) comfy or (b) beautiful. If a piece of clothing doesn't fall into one of those categories, throw it out.

Right up alongside my insecurity problem has been my frugal problem. I spent way too many years (like all my years) not buying clothes because I was cheap. Day after day, I tortured myself with clothes that didn't fit right, were out of style, or weren't made for my body type—all because I didn't want to buy new ones.

Ladies, our hearts and the love of our bodies are worth the cost. Please, by all means, join me in bargain shopping. I still don't spend big, but if I need a new pair of jeans, I get them. If my daughter puts on last year's pants and they no longer fit correctly, off to the store we go.

To know which clothes to purchase for myself and my daughter, I have had to become a student of my body and hers, studying them and asking myself, What kinds of clothes fit in all the right ways, and where can I get said clothes? We are all shaped differently, so what works for me will not work for my daughter. Try to be intentional and only go for the styles that work best and to the stores that sell them. And stay away from the places that don't! I cannot enter my pinkie toe into an American Eagle store without feeling insecure about my body. If I can avoid it, I do.

Last year was a big year for my girl. Her body began to make the changes from a girl to a young woman, and I was ready! This was the moment I had been training for. We had taken our normal jaunts between Justice and Children's Place when it happened— the whole changing room meltdown. Clothes came flying out above and thrown out below the door, accompanied by "None of these fit me!"

Girl, we have all been there. It's an opportunity to share, an opportunity to learn together. "Honey, there is nothing wrong with you just because these clothes don't fit right. Our bodies change and grow over time, and if these clothes no longer work, let's find a place where they do. It's not a bad thing that our bodies change; it is part of being a woman, and it is beautiful. Come on, let's figure out together where to go next."

This is where some momma diagnostics might come in handy. If your girl is struggling with her body in a way that she might not be able to articulate to you, do some investigating and praying to assess the reason why. Sherlock Momma to the rescue. Offer to take her shopping—and before you put the new clothes in her closet, take out and donate what no longer fits.

Out with the old, in with the new. And in a guilt-free, "it's perfectly normal that our bodies ebb and flow in and out of clothes" kind of way.

Focus on the Parts You Love

We all have parts about our bodies that we like, parts that we are kind of proud are ours and that make us feel thankful for the way God created us. It's okay, you can admit it. It's not bragging or prideful or arrogant but appreciative of God's creation. We all have a mental list containing the pieces of ourselves that we love. It's normal and okay that not all our parts show up on this list.

What is on your list? Have you ever thought about your body in this way? No, we are not the sum of our parts, but understanding the way we see ourselves surely does help when we look in the mirror. It gives us permission to focus on the parts of ourselves that we love—and be confident in loving them.

If you are anything like me, you look in the mirror and immediately see the parts you don't like. We home in on those bad boys for analysis and pray that something has miraculously changed in the past twenty-four hours.

Why do we do this to ourselves? Why do we constantly berate ourselves and walk a treadmill of self-shame? Maybe together we can stop, get off the treadmill of focusing on what we think needs changing, and instead focus on the parts we like and appreciate.

It's biblical, you know. Focusing on the positive is a biblical truth that will guard our hearts and bring us peace. Philippians 4:6–9 says:

> Do not be anxious about anything, but in every situation, by prayer and petition, with thanksgiving, present your requests to God. And the peace of God, which transcends all understanding, will guard your hearts and your minds in Christ Jesus.
>
> Finally, brothers and sisters, whatever is true, whatever is noble, whatever is right, whatever is pure, whatever is lovely, whatever is admirable—if anything is excellent or praiseworthy—think about such things. Whatever you have learned or received or heard from me, or seen in me—put it into practice. And the God of peace will be with you.

When worry or anxiety comes, what does God tell us to do? Bring it to him, and then take our mind off that and put it on something good. We don't need to fix the parts we don't like; we simply need not to pay attention to them anymore!

The next time you look in the mirror, go through the list in verse 8 in your mind. Which of my parts are noble? Pure? Lovely? Admirable? Excellent? Praiseworthy? May we focus on such things and may we gift our daughters the freedom that this brings. Let's give ourselves and our daughters permission to only see, look at, and pore over the parts of ourselves that we adore.

And ladies, young and old, when we look in the mirror and glance over our parts, may we be so bold as to even praise God for creating us so wonderfully.

Perhaps you have made the commitment to permanently rid your house of mirrors. This I fully support as it solves the issue altogether. My house has no full-length mirrors, only the smaller ones that typically come in bathrooms. If I want to see my full outfit, I have to stand on the edge of my bathtub. Each time I take that step up, the physical act of climbing reminds me to take captive my thoughts as I mirror gaze, give myself grace, and offer myself the difficult but ever rewarding perspective of body love.

Pamper Yo'Self

We are not all created to love pink frills; I was a sports girl myself. But through the years I have begun to appreciate whatever form of pampering makes me feel like a queen or a princess.

I don't think I am alone in feeling a twinge of enjoyment over spoiling myself; I just don't think we often give ourselves (or others) permission to be pampered in order to love how we look. It seems superficial and selfish. And it *is* if we make those things the center of our universe. But adding a little pampering to your days or weeks is an outward expression of the inward love we are growing for our bodies.

Here are a few thoughts on pampering:

- In the book of Esther, we learn that she had a yearlong pampering process before she became queen. If Esther gets a year, surely we can give ourselves and our daughters a day or two.
- When I asked a group of young women what makes them feel most confident, hands down the most popular answer was getting dressed up.
- We don't all have to pamper the same. My daughter hates fancy shoes. She is a Converse girl through and through. Whenever I try to get her a pair of fancies, she says to me, "You can buy those, but I won't wear them." Okay, so a cute pair of wedges and a cold-shoulder shirt probably won't be what makes her feel beautiful; they will be what makes her feel uncomfortable. As her mom, I've got to learn what does make her feel pampered.

Listed below are some options for pampering that come to mind; feel free to add to the list. I pray that you use it as a trial and error. Maybe go through each of them with your daughter over the course of a year. Cross out the ones that were blah for you and for her, and circle the ones that were fun and made you both feel lovely. Please don't make the same mistake I did and take way too long to make one or two of them a regular part of your lives. From the list, probably my favorite is getting my hair cut and colored. I am like a little schoolgirl on her way to the candy store; I literally skip through the door. I love changing up my hair color, and I promise you one of these days I will be brave enough to go all blue! (Someday, but not today.) I am thirty-six and have spent the entirety of my adult life getting this done only about once every couple years! I made excuses: it's too expensive, I don't have time, it's not really going to help, I'll feel guilty afterward, what if I make the wrong choice and it looks dumb?

Excuse, after excuse, after excuse kept me away from one of the most body-loving things I could do for myself. Can we ban the excuses? Can we teach our daughters to ban the excuses too and make pampering her a priority in the days and weeks ahead? (Insert picket signs and a rhythmic chant.) "Ban the Excuses, Love How You Look!"

Here we go, the list as promised:

- Get a manicure.
- Get a pedicure.
- Get a facial.
- Get your eyebrows waxed.
- Get your hair cut.
- Get your hair colored.
- Get some new makeup.
- Get a new accessory (watch, bracelet, ring, earrings, scarf, fedora—whatever floats your boat).

- Try a clothing service (LeTote is my favorite).
- Get a massage.
- Wear high heels out.
- Wear a dress.
- Wear something that sparkles.
- Get a body cream with a scent that you love.
- Find your "one and only, will never wear anything else again" perfume scent.
- Take a bubble bath—bath bomb, candles, music, and all (every once in a while, when Faith is having a long week, I draw her a bath like this, and it's golden).

What did I miss? Add a few others to the list:

_____

_____

_____

It's out of love and respect for ourselves that we treat our bodies like they are special. There is no one else on the entire earth exactly like us, and we should give our parts and pieces the special love and attention they deserve. A woman's body is an amazing thing; we were created to be beautifully taken care of.

My favorite vision of this is in a picture of my daughter and my husband on their way to a father-daughter dance. Faith's hair was gently pulled up on one side with cascading curls down the other side and perfectly placed glittering bobby pins throughout. She had glitter sprayed from head to toe, and her beautiful blue gown did the perfect swirling motion when she twirled. I caught a picture of them right as my husband was leaning down to whisper in her ear, "Faith, you look absolutely beautiful. I am so honored to be your daddy date tonight." The look on her face was coy confidence. You could see it in her smile; she believed what Daddy said to her was true because she felt it about herself too.

Isn't that what we all want? We know our beauty lies in greater things, deeper things that no size or scale can touch. But neither does the size or scale need to dictate our ability to feel beautiful, lovely, and stunning.

Sister of mine, it's okay to start treating yourself like you love how you look. Even better? Take your daughter along with you on the journey.

From an Expert on Body Love

God is so good to give us just the friends we need just when we need them. I was a scared new college girl, launched into a place where I knew no one, when Carrie bounced into my life. She was confident, wise, and just the friend this young, insecure girl needed. I could write entire books about the enormity of the ways God has shaped our friendship through the years (including both coming to Christ, though four years apart), but for the sake of this chapter we are going to focus on the "loving how we look" part.

My insecurity always baffled Carrie, and I loved that about her. While I complained about my looks, she carried herself with confidence. While I whined about my pants not fitting, she raved about her love for Old Navy. While I spent ridiculous amounts of time analyzing my appearance in front of a mirror, Carrie drew a pick through her hair, did a quick air guitar dance, and headed out. I learned so much from being her friend.

So it is with honor and joy that I pick Carrie's brain with you. It is the brain of a woman God shaped differently than me but who has soaked up all the full goodness of the truth that there is no beauty that is one size fits all.

Here is my interview with Carrie.

Q: When you look in the mirror, what do you see?

A: Physically, I see my face first, a pretty smile and pretty eyes, and I've always liked the dimples on my cheeks God gave me. Sometimes I think I look tired and sometimes I feel like my chin makes my face look too round and I think things like *I need to cut back on the processed food* or *I need to drink more water*. As I get older, I notice just a few little things that old people talk about—one gray hair that sticks out right in the front bang area that I secretly wish would turn into a streak like Rogue from *X-Men*. But overall, I don't feel like I look any older or different from what I did in college.

If I'm looking in a full-length mirror, I'm checking out what I'm wearing and trying not to notice the one area I'm most self-conscious of: my waistline. That's my Achilles' heel. Honestly, I just try to wear things that hide it. Sometimes I'm successful and sometimes I'm not, but most times I just don't dwell on it.

Q: Through the years, what has helped you to truthfully love the body that God gave you?

A: I do understand that God has given me a gift, and I am often thankful that I don't have a low self-esteem. I think over the years I've done things and challenged myself to things like running a full marathon. I do them to prove it's not the number on the scale that holds you back.

And it's also not the number on the scale that shows your overall health. I had a recent battle with a potential insurance company that couldn't believe that at my weight (which disqualified me from the originally quoted price range) I *actually* ran a full 26.2-mile marathon. I talked to three different managers who repeated over and over that they couldn't believe it, but "good for me" (eye roll).

I really do chalk it up to the way God made me. He really did give me the gift to not worry and dwell on size, as I know some women do, even before I had Jesus in my life. What was cool was that after I was saved I could start making sense of it through Scripture: "Take captive every thought" (2 Cor. 10:5); "As he thinks in his heart, so is he" (Prov. 23:7 NKJV); "Do not conform to the pattern of this world, but be transformed by the renewing of your mind" (Rom. 12:12). I think we have the power to choose what to think about, so let's use that power for good!

Q: How do you fight off negativity toward your shape and size?

A: I think that I focus on the truth. Could I lose a few pounds? Absolutely. (Reminder to self—get back on that. Eat a salad. Don't stop at McDonald's for dinner tonight.) But I don't associate my worth with my weight. It is a mind over matter thing, and I don't want to waste the time or energy it takes to feel bad.

Q: Do you do any practical things that help you feel beautiful?

A: My nephews make me feel good when they see me putting on eye makeup. Most recently, Sam asked if I was putting on makeup to look beautiful for his baptism. I said, "Yes! Is it working?" to which he replied, "Yep." So, even though I don't wear a lot of makeup, when I put on mascara I feel beautiful. I feel beautiful when I'm around my girls and we get dressed up to go somewhere. As mushy as it sounds, I feel beautiful when my man puts his arms around me, his touch, how he loves me makes me feel awesome, really good, womanly.

Q: What would you say to a young woman who struggles to feel beautiful because she feels too big?

A: I think I would tell her my story. It becomes so trite to keep saying "God loves you the way you are" (even though it is true). My identity is in the One True King, and I want to be healthy to be able to continue to do the work he has in store for me. But the Bible never talks about a number on the scale!

I'd ask her to take a look at the people she surrounds herself with. What does she notice about them? Does she notice more physical attributes or personality traits? Chances are, her friends are different shapes from her too. But she still loves them, finds them worthy, and appreciates different things about each one! Take that in.

Confident Mom
CHALLENGE

Challenge #9: This challenge is a multiple-choice challenge! Pick one of the following experiments to run with your daughter:

Experiment Option #1: Ten times a day for one week, say to yourself in the mirror, "I am beautiful."

Experiment Option #2: Go shopping together! For every item you bring home, donate an old one.

Experiment Option #3: Sit down with your daughter and name, out loud and possibly awkwardly, each part of your body that you love. Want to go the extra step? Talk about why you love that part so much. What function does it serve? What strength does it offer you?

Experiment Option #4: Take a look at the list of pampering options and pick at least two to do.

Bonus Challenge: Do all the experiments! Do one a week over the course of a month.

Confident Daughter
DISCUSSION QUESTIONS

1. If you could write a story about a confident mom and a confident daughter, what would your characters be like?

2. Take turns saying out loud, "I love how I look." How did that feel to say out loud? Why do you think it felt that way?

3. Have you ever been hard on yourself because a piece of clothing did not feel right on you? Share that time.

4. What kinds of clothing do you most like to wear? What types of clothes make you feel most beautiful?

5. Do you think it's okay to love some of our parts more than others? Why or why not?

6. What parts of yourself do you love the most?

7. How can we do a better job of focusing on the things we love when we look in the mirror?

8. If you were a queen or a princess, with the entire kingdom at your fingertips, what would your pampering routines look like?

9. Do you like getting dressed up? Why or why not?

10. If you could do one thing to pamper your body every single week, what would it be?

11. What are some changes you can make to treat your body like you love how you look?

A Mom's Prayer

Father, we are going to take a brave step today and thank you for the way we look. Thank you for the way you made us, which is like no one else on this entire earth. We pray that you would help us to be more positive about ourselves. We confess to you that it sounds awkward to say, "I love how I look." We have been trained to self-loathe rather than give praise where praise is due. We praise what you have made in us because when you took the time to create us, our looks were a part of your plan. We thank you, Lord! We thank you that when you chose our parts you did not make a mistake. Help us, God, to see ourselves the way you do: beautiful and wonderfully made. Amen.

ten

Our Jesus and Our Joy

I am so proud of you. You have dug in, you have persevered, and you have committed to the hard work of growing confident for the sake of your daughter. Well done, friend. You are almost there!

I'm sure that I have officially told you all of my secrets by now, but for fun I have one more Maria confession for you. Here it goes.

Something happens to me every time I hear a hip-hop song. The beat starts bumping and I cannot help myself. My hips start moving and I cannot make them stop. The superfly beats get me every single time. I can't help it, ladies, I just have to hit the floor. Have to.

Dancing has always been my joy. It frees me like not much else does. Give me some salsa, some ballroom dancing, some boot scootin' boogie, some flossing—I don't discriminate. When I dance, the worry shakes off. I laugh, I smile, and when I stop, I somehow feel free of the burdens I was carrying before.

Since I was a girl, dancing has been my joyful place. Why am I telling you this? You can imagine that this might have caused problems (for me and my parents) when I was a teenager. One needs to rein in one's booty shaking lest it communicate something you don't want it to, and so my joyful place warped into a place filled with shame and guilt and my outlet went away. Instead of dancing becoming a healthy, God-glorifying outlet, it became a secret one, one I felt I had to hide away and experience by myself.

I would have done well with some joy honing. It would have gone a long way with me for someone to speak into the places that made me come alive, teach me what on earth it had to do with Jesus, and then show me how to put the two together. The joy and Jesus combo.

The good news is that Jesus is pretty awesome. He can help our daughters and he can help us, because he always has good answers.

Sometime over the past decade, I learned that God is the one who created the dancing in me. God is the one who turns on the light switch of my heart every time that beat comes on, and I don't need to carry shame about it. What a confidence changer when I realized that Jesus didn't hate my dancing and that, in fact, my happiness was pleasing to him. That truth spoke the opposite of the insecurity I carried since I was a girl, and such freedom comes when we filter our joy through our Jesus.

We have the precious opportunity to help lead our girls in *their* joy—whatever it might be for them.

In this chapter we are going to end on a happy note. First, we are going to chat about the ways we can usher our girls toward Jesus. Then, we will talk about becoming a student of our daughters. What makes them smile? What makes them tick? What makes them overflow with laughter? Finally, we will bring the two together and offer our daughters ways to fulfill their joy through Jesus.

Let's go, this one is going to be fun!

Come to Me

I was twenty years old when I read the following words for the first time, and they changed my aching heart forever: "Come to me, all you who are weary and burdened, and I will give you rest. Take my yoke upon you and learn from me, for I am gentle and humble in heart, and you will find rest for your souls. For my yoke is easy and my burden is light" (Matt. 11:28–30). It was a few short months after I had given my life to Jesus. I was on a Campus Crusade for Christ retreat, and we were having "quiet time." I was such a brand-new baby Christian, and I found my first love in Matthew 11:28.

Was what God said true? Could Jesus really do that for me? Would he really take my weary and burdened soul and give me rest? Because there was one thing I knew for certain—I was extremely wearied and burdened. Carrying insecurity felt like a ton of bricks in your backpack. Every decision was a painful one, every sentence from another person was one to superanalyze, and every glance in the mirror sent me away discouraged. I was tired of carrying that burden. I was so weary from fighting against myself all the time. It is a terrible battle when the one person you want to run away from is yourself.

If you have carried insecurity, I believe you can relate. Our daughters can too; their backpacks are filling up as they grow— one brick at a time.

I wonder sometimes what my life would have been like if I had asked Jesus to come into my life earlier. What it would have been like for Matthew 11:28 to wash over me at the age of ten or thirteen or sixteen. What a relief that would have been to me. But I trust God with the fact that my wearied journey set me on a ferocious quest to give to my daughter what I did not have: *rest for her soul*.

Jesus is her greatest hope, and we have until she is eighteen to teach her about him.

So many other things in our daughters' lives will be louder, more frequent, and more intense. The friends, the boys, the school, the activities, and the screens. All pining for her attention, all battling for her spirit. Each and every one of those things wants the best part of her and the most of her. We have eighteen years to jump up and down with passion, hope, and joy and to remind her daily: "Sweet daughter! Don't forget about Jesus. The one who died to save you. No matter what comes in and out of your day, no matter how life hits you, remember he is always there with you. Jesus wants to help you carry your load; don't forget to take him with you today."

May we bring Jesus to her mind through daily reminders, weekly church attendance, yearly mission trips—whatever it takes and all the time. And may we go back to Matthew 11:28 ourselves when we grow weary of reminding her.

The truth is we can do everything right. We can nail the confidence modeling, throw out our mirrors and scales forever, serve only the most delicious and nutritious food for every meal, speak only encouraging words, and it will all fall short without faith in Christ. God and God alone is in the business of lasting soul change.

I realize that not everyone believes that to be true, and you and your family might still be searching out what you believe about Jesus. You still might be figuring out the role you desire faith to have in your family. And that's totally okay. I know that if you are searching for God, he will find you.

That's the best thing about Jesus. He doesn't need to be sold to you, or to convince you, or to force you. He simply is, and he always will be.

As a mom, it is unnerving that there isn't much I can say to my children with complete confidence or without hesitation. As a momma who lost a baby, I realized years ago that I cannot protect my children from pain. Or stop it from coming. Or be there all the time for all things. But I can give them Jesus. I can show them the power of healing he has had in my life, I can model for them how sweet it is to have solid truth to build my life on, and I can teach them what Jesus has taught me. It feels so good to be able to give them something so solid, so reliable, and so beyond a shadow of a doubt.

Matthew 11:28 is a promise. When we come to him and give him our burdens, he takes them from us. When we go to him, we see that he is gentle and humble in heart. Quickly we notice that Jesus is a soft and sweet place to land. Then, in return, he offers us something. Jesus reaches his hand out to us, but notice he does not force us to take it. Verse 29 says, "Take my yoke upon you." We must make the choice to take Jesus's burden in exchange for our own. Our daughters need to make this choice for themselves too. And then what do we see? We see that we just traded in a burden as heavy as ten mack trucks and in its place received a load as light as feathers. In that moment, we find rest for our souls.

This is a daily promise God makes to us; promises are a wonderful gift to offer to our girls. We cannot promise them much, but we can affirm the promise in Matthew 11:28 with full confidence.

What this looks like in your family is entirely up to you. I pray, fellow momma, that prayer over your daughter, for your daughter, and on behalf of your daughter becomes a regular part of your days and weeks. I pray that you find the courage to offer her Jesus in many places. If we persevere through anything, may we persevere through this.

Class Is in Session

I heard this on the radio when my kids were babies, and it stuck to me like glue: "Become a student of your children. Study them."

Hmm, like a spy? Like a momma ninja hiding around corners with a notebook and pen, taking notes on all of their antics? Or like a kid with pigtails and glasses sitting at a desk and the topic being taught on the board is the best topic ever: in big white letters on the chalkboard it says your daughter's name?

Can you tell I have had some fun with this one?

It is so golden! Learning is a one-way gig. The teacher teaches, you listen. Sure, every so often you get to insert yourself with a question or an answer, but for the most part the teacher gives the information and the students receive it.

How strange to think of ourselves as the students and our daughters as the teachers. Grab your notebook, your favorite pen, and watch and listen.

We mommas love us some words, am I right? I love to tell my daughter things, ask her things, tell her some more things, and then (ahem) tell her what to do.

As we venture into talking about what brings our daughters joy, listen and observe.

No words.

No opinions.

No questions.

Just learning.

Something has got to bring your daughter joy. And let's be honest, growing up is hard. Middle school and high school can be brutal. But we can be the joy police in our homes and usher our daughters into situations that bring them laughter, joy, and happiness.

But first we have to learn about her in order to be able to help her know where to go to find joy. Why? Because we all have our places of joy.

Mine is having dance parties in the living room and loud karaoke in the car.

My husband's is having a day of golf or tennis.

My daughter's is drawing and listening to her music.

My one son's is playing football.

My other son's is fishing.

And currently, my youngest son's is playing *Paw Patrol*.

We all have our joy places.

What does your daughter *love*? What brings her peace, laughter, or rest? What brings out the best version of herself? What is her go-to activity or passion?

Following are some possibilities, but you may have more to add. Let's brainstorm a bit. Circle all that may apply.

Art

Dancing

Sports

Horseback riding

Reading

Makeup tutorial videos

Hair tutorial videos

Any tutorial videos

Making TikTok videos

Tweaking her Instagram posts just right

Making slime

Cooking

Watching movies

Netflix bingeing

Photography

Fashion

Resist the temptation to ask her; instead, just watch her. Maybe over the course of a week or a month, go on your own spy investigation. Once you have it, you are ready for the next section in which we'll bring it all together—our Jesus and our joy.

Good Girls Gone Wild

There is *joy* and then there is *wild*. Earlier in the book, we talked about the fact that the logic and reasoning part of the brain is not yet fully developed in a young woman. She's got the emotional part down pat, but the reasoning part is still growing. We were all teens once; this was our story too.

Here's the thing. As parents, we walk a fine line between condemning and pushing our daughters away on the one hand and guiding and drawing them in to listen on the other hand. When we seek to offer them our wisdom, may our motivation be this: taking what we have learned about them and showing them the healthiest path to take.

I told you how I loved to dance. Well, this girl loved some "all ages dance clubs" when I was a teen. Would my parents allow this? No, of course not. So, what did I do? "Hey, Mom and Dad, I'm going to Clara's house." And then I went clubbing. Did I love the constant booty bumping? Not really, but I was an emotional teen and didn't know what I know today, and that was the only place I knew where I could dance. Just for joy, just for fun, and not for competition or winning.

So, what does being a student of our daughters look like? It is noticing an outlet in our girls, seeing what makes them come alive, and offering them constant and healthy opportunities to do this.

My husband has an excellent example of this from when he was young. Dave has always been a sports guy; he loves playing them, watching them, analyzing them, and hearing about them. For him the order is God, family, sports. When Dave was in middle school, he had a severe leg injury from a four-wheeling accident in which he nearly lost his leg. It set back his entire high school sports career, but he had such drive and passion. He loved football, but was playing football the only route for him? His parents wondered if there were other outlets he could take part in and got him set up in a refereeing and umpire program. His reffing career stayed with him well past college, and it provided some of his most joyous memories growing up. To this day, he is the best coach/referee in the entire world (and that is my completely unbiased opinion).

It is all about getting creative and naming the positive.

It's not "how dare you sit on that tablet all day" or "don't you know that clubbing is disgusting" or "why are you wasting your time with that?!" Side note: I should have been heavily punished for lying to my parents. But after a much-deserved consequence, a conversation like this would have helped: "Honey, I noticed that [insert your daughter's interest here] is something you love to do. I did some research and thought about it, and I was wondering if you would like to try out [insert creative genius parenting idea here]."

I wasn't a bad girl. All the many times I felt that I failed at making good life choices only added to my insecurities. But when emotions are our main guide, it's no wonder we wander off in the wrong direction. My prayer is that we can help show our girls that their interests, hobbies, and desires to have fun are not inherently wrong or bad. But there are the best choices and the not *at all* best choices, and sometimes they need a little help finding out what those are.

Joy and Jesus

Did you know that God does not want us to be unhappy?

I didn't know this. I mean it sounds silly to say out loud, but if I am being honest, my own insecurities and self-criticism affected my view of God. I thought, *Surely if I am so down on myself, God must be too. Surely if I am so critical of myself, then God must be too.*

No and no. Jennifer Dukes Lee says it best in her book *The Happiness Dare*: "Here is the truth that no one told us (or at least that no one told me): *Happiness isn't the opposite of holy. It's a part of what makes you holy.* Happiness isn't the opposite of joy. It's a part of Christ-inspired joy, expressed within you. Happiness isn't selfish or stupid or wrong or ridiculous. When we seek it, we are more, not less, like Jesus."[1]

Teaching our daughters that their joy is pleasing to Jesus is a holy pursuit. Imagine the impact we can have on our girls' confidence if we teach them at a young age that it is good to pursue the things that make them most joy-filled.

It is so tenderly sweet to be known by someone. God knows us well, and he knows that we will need his joy to sustain us through the rocky terrains of this life. You know your daughter; now is the time you get to share what you've learned with her.

I get goosebumps picturing this unfolding in your home. You walk up to your girl and share with her what you learned as you studied her. With gentleness, compassion, and love, you utter something like this: "Honey, I notice that you love watching makeup tutorial videos [or drawing, art, photography, fashion]. I notice that it makes you smile and brings you joy, and that you seem happy when you are doing it. I think you like it because God created a gift in you, something special in you! You are creative, you are fun, you are a talented artist, and I would love to learn more about this thing that you love so much. Would you show me?"

To a daughter who loves dancing, sports, hiking, or anything active, you might say, "Honey, I notice that you come alive when you are on the sports field [or dancing, in nature, being physical]. I think you are amazing, and I think God has given you a gift. You are so strong, determined, and passionate, and I love how you smile and laugh when you are doing this activity. Is there any way I can do this with you once or twice?"

Believe it or not, as a teen, as much as I pushed my parents away, I would have died and gone to heaven if they offered to do a dance class with me. Some of my favorite memories with my dad growing up were swing dancing to Glenn Miller in our living room or having dance parties as a family when we were on vacation. More of that, please. Way more. Show your daughter that her joy is important to you and important to God, not just once in a while but consistently every week or every month.

Trust me, even as I write to you my heart is being challenged. Life goes by so fast. It is busy and there is so much that has to be done. How on earth can I make time for all this? Friend, I assure you that we have *not* been failures up to this point. We are not done, our chances are not at an end, and there is no benefit in carrying guilt for the time that has already passed.

But today is a new day, and our tool belts are full. Adding joy to our repertoire of ways to help our girls makes it one that we can pull out in case of an emergency. We notice she is down, having a hard week, month, or year. We have things that we cannot just say but do:

- We can pray for her every night, for God to draw close to her, for God to comfort her in her pain, and for God to send rescue.
- We can offer her times to be with Jesus—go to church, find a local youth group event, go to a concert, set her up for coffee with a trusted mentor or Jesus-loving friend.
- We can remind her of all the things we see to be true about her. Not just in her beauty, but how she is wired. We can bring her focus back to what brings her joy, reminding her that these areas that make her happy are good places for her to focus in on.
- We can make the joy places happen! When she is down or out or weary, go do the happy things. Sit in her room and watch hours of the silly videos she loves, go on a hunt to all the popular places to take Instagram shots, draw her a bath, set up her Eno hammock in the backyard where she can draw, rest, or listen to music.

I know. Sometimes it is going to be like carrying a porcupine. I feel you, sister. When our girls are hurting, we are top on the list of people to take it out on. May you treat yourself to the same list we made for your daughter.

- Pray for yourself.
- Go be with Jesus.
- Remember that God created you to enjoy your joyful places.
- Go do some happy things.

And enter back into the battle with your daughter strong and ready. I promise, someday when she is older and she holds her own baby child in her arms for the very first time, she will come back and thank you.

It's all worth it.

From an Expert at Being a Teenager

Taylor Howard is an expert at being thirteen years old. She personifies everything I remember from that age. Taylor loves to hang with friends, she is funny and fun to be around, and of course she pushes back on her parents every now and again. I love her perseverance. Being thirteen is hard, right? Things don't go as planned with friends, parents are forced to take things away because of "that" tone of voice, and mistakes are made. We've all lived through it. But through the years, I have watched Taylor respond to hard situations and allow them to teach her.

Taylor and her mom, Cammie, do this awesome thing that I love (I have totally stolen the idea from them to do with my daughter). They write notes back and forth to each other. I love this because feelings are sometimes hard to articulate out loud. Writing them down not only takes away some of the pressure but also makes for an excellent keepsake. Check out this sweet one from Taylor to her mom:

> Mom, I also had a great time Monday. Thank you for being so generous, and I think getting caught in the rain made it more of an adventure! Thank you for taking the whole day off to spend time with me. That was very sweet. I had a great day! Also, I enjoyed doing face masks together and watching my shows (even tho they were weird lol). I love you! Love, Tay (and all we moms wipe our eyes)

Here is Taylor's thirteen-year-old perspective on joy and Jesus:

Q: How has your relationship with Jesus impacted you as you navigate all that comes with being a teen?

A: I remind myself that God loves me no matter what people think and that he's always there for me when I feel alone or stressed out.

Q: What brings you joy? What types of things make you smile and laugh?

A: I love hanging out with my good friends and watching funny shows with them and just being crazy.

Q: What does it mean to you when your parents take an interest in the things that you love? How does it make you feel?

A: It's great because I know that they care about me and want to spend time with me.

Q: Do you go to church regularly? How does it help you?

A: Yes, I go to church almost every week, and I like that it's at the beginning of the week because it gives me a good reminder of how I want to live and treat others.

Q: What helps you when you are tempted to compare yourself to other girls around you?

A: I try to remember that God created me exactly how he wanted me to be, and I'm perfect the way I am.

Q: What are your goals for yourself over the next four years? What do you want for your life?

A: I want to have a stronger relationship with God, build stronger relationships with my friends, and try not to get into drama.

Q: What helps you feel confident?

A: Being around my good friends, who build me up and encourage me.

Confident Mom
CHALLENGE

Challenge #10: Find what brings you joy. We all have something we love to do. Find yours, find your daughter's, and *do them*! Whatever they are—no matter how silly, embarrassing, or public—just do them.

Bonus Challenge: Spoil yourself. Please? Just this once? Guilt-and-shame-free, go do that thing you love that you never allow yourself to do. You have been digging through this book, and it is hard. You are working on all these things for your daughter, but you need some loving too. Go ahead, pull out your scheduler and put it on the calendar.

Confident Daughter
DISCUSSION QUESTIONS

1. What makes you laugh—that giddy giggle that is so contagious?
2. What kinds of activities make you feel the most like yourself? What makes you come alive and feel free?
3. If you could do anything on a Saturday afternoon, what would you do?

4. Galatians 5:1 says, "It is for freedom that Christ has set us free. Stand firm, then, and do not let yourselves be burdened again by a yoke of slavery." Insecurity often feels like slavery; Christ came so that we can be free of it. What do you think about that?

5. What do you think about Jesus, and what role does he have in your life?

6. What are ways you can include Jesus in your daily or weekly routine?

7. Why do you think Jesus cares about our joy?

8. What is the difference between happiness that causes us to drift away from God (for example, being mean to someone may feel good in the moment, but it doesn't please Jesus) and happiness that causes us to draw closer to him?

9. Mom, how can you help your daughter have more joy in her life?

10. Daughter, how can you help your mom have more joy in her life?

A Mom's Prayer

Father, we confess to you now that we can spend so much time being hard on ourselves that we sometimes forget how much our joy pleases you. Not only joy of this world, though you have given us these things for our blessing, but also joy in you. God, would you help us to lead our daughters toward joy in you with reckless abandon? May we have the courage to not be ashamed and to constantly lift high your name, to offer you as a solution time and time again. If we have somehow stripped joy from our home, I pray you would forgive us. Help us, Lord, to fight for joy in our families and to make time for laughter and happiness and fun. This life is so hard sometimes. Pain, insecurity, and fear can attack us from so many different angles that we are sometimes overwhelmed. Father, would you reign supreme over all of these things in our hearts and in our homes? And when we lay our head on our pillow each night, may we focus on our joy and our Savior. Amen.

eleven

Beauty from Ashes

My Mom's Perspective

O h, Chris, it's a girl!" Mike said, beaming as he looked at me. He stroked my face and looked back at our sweet gift. Immediately, hopes and dreams flooded my head: being a princess, painting nails, combing hair, playing dress-up, relating to someone, and having a happy-go-lucky home for her to grow up in. Nothing was more exciting and scarier than being handed Maria. She was sweet, small, and best of all, mine. I remember my motherly protectiveness kicking in within the first ten minutes of her life as the nurse placed drops in her eyes so she could see well. I didn't want her long, manicured fingernails hurting my little girl's sweet, naive new eyes. Little did I know that those sweet baby eyes would one day see herself as less than what God intended.

As I held her in those early days, touched her head and held her tiny hands, my hopes and dreams were clouded by doubt and unanswerable questions. *How am I going to do this? How do I be a mom? What if she gets sick? What if I pass on my fears to her? What if I fail? What if? What if?* Being excited and scared about being a mom wasn't the only thing that happened at that time. A worrisome and insecure nature began to grow in me. Like many other moms, I wanted to protect my girl from the evils of this world and prevent any of life's difficulties that I faced. I was so afraid I wouldn't be able to give her what I didn't think I had to give.

Growing up in my family had its challenges, with splashes of joy mixed in. My problem was that in my early years, the difficulties outweighed the joys, and I became a person who has a hard time finding the joy and the hope in life's situations. I decided to hold everything in and process what was going on in my own way instead of talking it out or seeking help. Anything to avoid making waves. I guess for all of us, it is easier to look back and figure things out than to know what to do when we are in the middle of doing life. Looking back, I can see how I started people pleasing early on. Because of fear, I was often paralyzed to take a stand on what I knew was right. In the craziness of life and at about the same time the fears began, God placed faith inside of me. Something happened in me that made me believe. I remember believing without a doubt that God existed and that he loved me. I attended church all the time with my mom, dad, brother, and sister. As time went on, God was the only Rock I had to hold on to when everything else in my life seemed to fail me. He was the one I started turning to with my fears and tears.

My teenage years were tough. I didn't at all like what I saw when I looked in the mirror. I was a lonely, quiet, insecure, overweight, and fearful teenager. Many times I cried, wanting God to take me home to escape my life. I recall looking in the mirror and telling myself how worthless I was, and if God made mistakes, I was one of them. I used to think I was ugly and pounded my thighs because they stuck out too much. I thought maybe if I was better, people would love me more or not be so mean to me. My imperfections became reasons I was not treated well. I became what I call a comparer. I looked at other girls, quickly compared myself to them, and then decided if I envied them or hated myself more because of the way they looked. Most of the time, I came out on the bottom.

When I was sixteen, God began to change me. I attended a retreat at which in the depth of my soul I began to actually feel God's love for me instead of just knowing he did. God reached down and touched this unhappy girl and gave me hope. The teenage years continued to be tough, and many were filled with anger, fights, fear, and hurt. But through it all, Mom and Dad stayed together, and it was good for a while to feel better. Then I was off to college. The tight limits and boundaries were gone, and I was on my own. In college I became more of a follower and did what everyone else was doing in order to fit in and feel like I belonged.

Three years into college, and after a few years of making mistakes with drinking and guys, I met my future husband, Mike. I quickly fell in love. There was something about him that I thought would rescue me from my home, with its struggles, and rescue me from me. It didn't hurt that he looked great in his Navy uniform.

Early in our relationship, we defined it as being designed by God. There were so many similarities in our families, our parents, and our faith that we were bound for the altar regardless of the past. We did all the right things. He asked my dad for my hand, we were blessed by the priest, we attended the premarital weekend, we prayed together, and we got married within one year of knowing one another. Three months following our wedding, we packed up what little we had and moved across the country and away from our families. Shortly after we arrived in a new place, our true natures kicked in. My insecurities and poor self-esteem, coupled with his anger and controlling personality, set us up for conflict.

But what also began to kick was our little baby growing inside of me. As it turned out, I was pregnant when we got married. I was naive and thought my missed period was from the stress that came from college finals, planning a wedding, and my family issues. I didn't even consider the idea that I could be pregnant. It was on the cross-country drive that the newest adjective was added to my list of insecurities: ashamed.

Fast-forward to where we began this chapter. I am now a mother of a beautiful baby girl. I am holding her and wondering how to be a mom and how to protect her from not only the world around her but also all the weaknesses of her father and myself. Needless to say, when I got married and began a family, my life tool belt was a bit empty. I didn't know that it wasn't all up to *me* to keep her protected. I wasn't able to allow God to do that or to give me the strength to be a mom. I had not lost my belief in God, but my faith was weak. I somehow put more faith in my inabilities and Mike's controlling nature than in the power of God to help us overcome.

You've read about Maria's struggles with insecurity and self-image, and now you understand where she got them. It was a strange feeling; I could see what was happening but felt totally paralyzed to be a positive influence on her and help her through it all. I wanted desperately to be a mom who played with her and spent hours talking and laughing with her, but worry and taking care of things took the place of those—another layer of shame. My insecurities as a woman, wife, and mom were passed on to Maria. Many times, I watched her struggle, yet I was speechless, which came from an inability to speak up for myself as well as not having the wisdom to give. I hadn't conquered my own battle with insecurity, so I felt totally unequipped to help with hers.

We were one of those families that, from the outside, looked like we had it all together, but at home we struggled. I remember thinking that there were hundreds of books for pregnancy, childbirth, first year, second year, toddler, and so on, but where was the book to help navigate adolescence? Where was the help for the insecurity baggage I carried? Where was help when I needed it most?

It is my deepest prayer that you would know there is always *hope*. I have learned that God is a redeemer. There is always time for a second chance. As adults, Maria and I have developed the relationship I dreamed of when I held her as a baby. It is such a wonderful blessing to me. God's hand has always been on Maria,

God's hand has always been on me, and God's hand is assuredly on you and your daughter too.

Once God got ahold of me and began teaching me about how he sees me, I was able to talk to Maria and work through much of what she went through and what we went through with her. Our God is so good. He has brought our family out of the darkness and into the light, which means that all the stuff that kept us from growing and maturing in our faith was brought out into the open and talked about. We began communicating with one another, and we were able to seek healing and offer forgiveness. Now that our hearts are empty of the ugly stuff, there is room for God's hope and joy.

God can do the same in your family too. He can bring healing, forgiveness, and hope. He can turn any road you are on into a road that leads to redemption. It is never too late. For Maria and me, it happened when she was in her twenties. But for you? Maybe it can start today.

I wish I knew then what I know now. What I want to encourage you to do is to have hope and not give up on yourself or your daughter! God never gave up on us. What my husband and I lacked in our parenting skills, God made up for. All those character traits Maria had growing up that caused me to believe she wanted nothing to do with me, like her strong-willed personality and her defiance, God turned around for good. Her determination and unwillingness to budge is now for Christ. She is bold, and her faith in Christ is strong. Genesis 50:20 says, "You intended to harm me, but God intended it for good to accomplish what is now being done, the saving of many lives."

If I could go back in time and be where you are, these are the things I would do differently.

Be honest. Be honest with your daughter. Make the time to take her to lunch, get a pedicure, or go to coffee, and it will help build bridges of communication. If talking is difficult, try writing in a journal to each other. Just be honest, and don't forget to tell her you love her. She is worth the extra effort. Even when she is screaming, "I hate you," she is really screaming for love and attention. Be honest if you struggle with your own self-image. Maybe together you can help build each other up. A shopping day to help keep Mom trendy is always fun.

Have hope. I found such comfort in Psalm 126:5–6:

> Those who sow with tears
> > will reap with songs of joy.
> Those who go out weeping,
> > carrying seed to sow,
> will return with songs of joy,
> > carrying sheaves with them.

I found such hope in God's promise that all the tears I had shed from a poor self-image and shame and the sadness over Maria's difficulties he could turn into joy. When Maria turned twenty, so much turned around. The sheaves I now carry are my eight beautiful grandchildren. He restores, he redeems, he saves, and he loves. In Joel 2:25, God tells us, "I will repay you for the years the locusts have eaten." And he has done just that. After many years of hardship and struggle, the life and relationship God has given us is beyond what I could have ever dreamed of. Have hope.

Trust. Another thing I would have done differently is to trust my gut. There were many times I wanted to say no, but I didn't out of fear or worry. Little did I know that *no* is exactly what Maria needed to hear. At times, being too lenient to avoid arguments wasn't the best for Maria. Trust God. Proverb 3:5–6 says,

> Trust in the LORD with all your heart
> > and lean not on your own understanding;
> in all your ways submit to him,
> > and he will make your paths straight.

Pray. Pray without ceasing. First Thessalonians 5:16–18 teaches, "Rejoice always, pray continually, give thanks in all circumstances;

for this is God's will for you in Christ Jesus." There were times when all I could do was pray. In my early prayers, I was a pleader: "Oh please, God, don't let anything happen to her. Oh God, keep her safe. Oh God, please don't let her get hurt. Oh God, please don't let her turn out like me." God is faithful, and he kept her safe in his way, in his arms. Life wasn't easy, but he was faithful to us. I began reading Scripture to help me be a better mom, and that is when I really learned how to pray over my children. At night, once they were fast asleep, I would go into their rooms and kneel at their bedsides. I would lay my hand over their sleeping heads and pour out my heart to God. I loved them and wanted so much for God to be in their lives, but I knew I couldn't do it without him. So both my children were handed over to God. My heart would cry out to God as I wept over them. I sought forgiveness as well as God's will in their lives and mine.

Another way I began to pray for my children was to insert their name in whatever Scripture passage I read. For example, as I read Colossians 1:9–13 aloud, each time the word *you* occurred I inserted Maria or Nick, depending on whom I was praying for. I encourage you to pray over your children using Scripture and with the belief that God will do what he says he will do.

Love. I think we all love our kids. God created us that way. But as they grow, they need our love to grow with them. We need to teach our children about not only how much we love them but also how much God loves them and how he sees us. We need to believe this for ourselves too. I think if that knowledge had been in my parent tool belt, I might have been able to replace some of the lies I used to believe about myself with what God says about me. I trust that God brought me into a deeper relationship with him in my forties so that I too could learn how he sees me and could walk with Maria as she learned how he sees her, as well as teach it to my grandchildren. A verse that I now hold close to my heart on the days I struggle with shame and doubt is Zephaniah 3:17:

The LORD your God is with you,
  the Mighty Warrior who saves,
He will take great delight in you;
  in his love he will no longer rebuke you,
  but will rejoice over you with singing.

Picture that. God, who put the stars in the sky, sings over you. We love our kids like that, and sometimes we moms need to remember he does the same for us.

I wish I had believed back then that Maria loved me. I too often translated her defiance, harsh words, arguments, or door slams as lack of love. I was wrong. Have faith that your daughter loves you and wants to have a relationship with you based on unconditional love. Jesus loves us that way. Romans 5:8 says, "But God demonstrates his own love for us in this: While we were still sinners, Christ died for us."

We can demonstrate God's love to our daughters when we love them through their sin and do not turn our backs on them or give up on them. There is so much vying for their hearts and attention. They need their mom to step in and love them and make time to let them know that.

Forgive. While waiting at a local pizza restaurant in 2004, the words "I'm so sorry, Mom" were spoken to me by Maria. To this day, as I recall that sweet, unexpected moment, my eyes tear up because I never thought those words would be spoken. I had no hesitation in offering Maria forgiveness. A moment like this is what we moms hope for.

The other side of forgiveness for me was seeking forgiveness from God for my own sins while raising Maria. When I allowed God's grace to fall on me, it was easier to extend it to Maria. Our daughters are looking to us to see what forgiveness looks like. They might not say it, but they are watching us. They are watching how we act, speak, love, argue, forgive, or resent. They are taking in all we do like a sponge. They might not even realize they are doing it, but it gets tucked away in their memory and will surface, for good or bad, when they are wives and moms.

Get help. We can't do it alone. God placed your daughter in your home for you to be her mom. If you are really struggling with how to manage the teenage years, do everything you can to get some help. Talk to other parents of teenage girls, seek a Christian counselor, or talk to your pastor, youth group leader, or other women. It's a good thing to seek help, and it feels good to talk to other women about your girls. It will help you gain insight and get some good ideas on what you can do.

If you sense in your gut that something is not right with your daughter, seek wisdom and counsel. Your mom gut is usually right. Your daughter may say everything is okay just to get you to back off. But she needs you to see beyond her words and get her help because her life depends on it, and not only her life but also the lives of your grandchildren and future generations to come.

Your daughter needs you to be confident. We can do it. You can do it. No matter what your childhood was like and no matter what your relationship is right now with your daughter, she needs you. I thought I could manage alone; it wasn't until I accepted Christ as my Lord that I realized I needed help. And that's when it all changed for my family. He wants us to stay together and live out his will.

The great thing is that even when I didn't know him as I do today, he was still active in my life. No matter where you are in your faith today, salvation, grace, mercy, and freedom can be yours too. I learned that it didn't matter what church I attended or my religion. What mattered was where I placed Christ in my life and in my heart. I needed a Savior.

If you have a tense relationship with your daughter and you don't have Christ in your life, maybe that's what he is calling you to today. Once he is part of your life, he will start to change you. All you have to do to make this happen is talk to him. Pray to God, admitting you need him, acknowledging that you have fallen short, accepting Christ's death and resurrection as powerful truth, and then asking God to reside at the center of your life. Then things will change with your daughter too.

If you already know Christ and your daughter is struggling, get together with friends and begin talking about what's going on in your daughters' lives and pray for them. God is active in all our lives. He wants us to join with him to raise our daughters.

I chose to call this chapter "Beauty from Ashes" because of the words of Isaiah 61. Early on, when I rededicated my life to Christ, I sat in a women's Bible study in which this chapter was taught. I cry today when I read it and see just how much God wants us to be whole. The way he fulfilled his promises was to send Jesus. I end with this, so you can see that your daughter needs you to believe that you are loved and that she is loved and that a great life awaits you both. You and your daughter are promised a true princess crown. Hurry, dear one, and believe.

> The Spirit of the Sovereign LORD is on me,
>> because the LORD has anointed me
>> to proclaim good news to the poor.
> He has sent me to bind up the brokenhearted,
>> to proclaim freedom for the captives
>> and release from darkness for the prisoners,
> to proclaim the year of the LORD's favor
>> and the day of vengeance of our God,
> to comfort all who mourn,
>> and provide for those who grieve in Zion—
> to bestow on them a crown of beauty
>> *instead of ashes*,
> the oil of joy
>> instead of mourning,
> and a garment of praise
>> instead of a spirit of despair.
>> (Isa. 61:1–3, emphasis added)

Confident Mom
CHALLENGE

Challenge #11: Go on a mother-daughter coffee or tea date to do this fun activity. Bring with you a bag of M&M's or Skittles (or any treat you both enjoy, but they have to be small and multicolored). Before you open the bag of yummies, read the description below and dive in.

Each color represents one of you. Go ahead. Pick one of each color that represents you.

Now take turns picking one piece at a time out of the bag, and as you do you will take turns sharing. When you pick out your color, share one thing that you *love* about yourself. When you pick out the other person's color, share one thing that you *love* about them. Repeat until your bag of treats is empty.

Bonus Challenge: Go meet with your own mom. Share with her all you have been digging through in this book—what has been hard, good, and easy. Share with her what it has brought up about your own childhood. If your mom is no longer living, I am so sorry. Maybe write it to her in the form of a letter. I pray that this challenge speaks to your heart with tenderness and gentleness.

Confident Daughter
DISCUSSION QUESTIONS

1. Part of our story sometimes includes the need to grieve when life has not gone the way we expected or hoped. Is there any part of your past or present that you have not allowed yourself to grieve over?

2. What thoughts ran through your mind the first time you held your daughter? How did her life change you? Share the story of the day she was born.

3. A crazy thing about being a parent is that so much is going on during your children's early years, years they don't usually

remember! What was life like for you when your daughter was little? Share some of life's ups and downs from that time.

4. Together, read back through the Scripture passages in this chapter. Which one stood out the most to each of you and why?

5. Isaiah 61:1 says that Jesus is coming to "proclaim freedom for the captives." Is there anything in your life that has taken you captive?

6. Christ came so that we could be free. Take a minute to pray for freedom for both of you.

7. Do you believe there is hope? Do you believe there is hope for a different future? What is your hope?

8. Mom, Daughter, have you given your life to Christ? If so, share with each other your story and consider making a rededication today. If not, what is stopping you?

A Mom's Prayer

A prayer from my mom's heart to ours:

Lord, thank you so much for our sweet, precious daughters. You are good, kind, and merciful, Lord, and we confess today that there are times when we struggle with being in relationship with them or we have said things that might have hurt them. Father, we ask for forgiveness and rest on your promise that when we are weak you are strong. Help us to be moms who are wise, kind, forgiving, and loving as you are to us. Lord, our prayer is that our daughters grow to be strong women who love you and truly see themselves as you see them—beautifully and wonderfully made. Lord, we ask for protection for them from the things of this world that fight against all that is good and pure. Help them to have eyes, ears, and a heart for things that are good. If there are any negative things already planted in their brain and heart toward themselves that are hurtful, we ask you to replace them with truths from your Word. May we speak words that will lift them up, may they have friends who encourage them, may they be a friend who encourages, and, Lord, may they know in the depths of their heart how much they are loved and cherished. We pray that we can draw them to you, and may someday they draw others to you. You are our hope! You are our anchor. You are our Father. You are truth and light. We look forward to the wonderful things you will do in our daughters' lives. We are humbled that you have called us to this job as their moms. May we journey together in raising them. Thank you, Lord, for all you have done and will do. We pray all these things in the name of your precious son, Jesus. Amen.

twelve

Letters from Our Daughters

I want you to hear from our daughters. I want you to hear their words, their hearts, and their thoughts.

I sit here with you, knowing it may be hard, but I ask you to read these words as if they are straight from the heart of your girl. I realize situations differ and the dynamics of our family relationships are not the same. But I believe it bodes well for us to hear from others who have gone before us, to hear straight from the mouths of the girls we are trying to love on, and to ask ourselves, *Does my own daughter feel this way too?*

In order to peek into the minds of daughters, early in 2018 I created a Confidence Survey and asked for anonymous responses. Women from ages eleven to fifty-four filled it out. I want to share some of their words with you. But instead of just listing their answers, I decided to write a series of letters based on what they said. I added transition words and punctuation; otherwise, the entirety of these letters is formed from their words.

These letters are summaries, jam-packed with the heart-wrenching answers these daughters gave to me. If something here grips you, highlight it or underline it and go back to it later. Ask yourself, *Why did this stand out to me?*

May we open up our hearts and our minds as if we were hearing straight from our daughters.

Letters from Our Girls

Mom writes:

Dear Daughter,

I was praying for you today, and I wondered if you would do me the honor of writing me a letter? I want to know how best to pray for you. To start, is there anything you would like to share with me? Anything that you want me to know but have never had the courage to tell me?

Daughter writes:

Dear Mom,

I want you to know that I struggle. I struggled a lot with my faith in middle school, and many times I find it hard to believe that there is a God who loves me. I also struggle with lack of confidence and low self-esteem. I've never wanted to tell you; I didn't want to give you more stress in your life or make you feel guilty.

I don't want you to worry about me, but I need to tell you that I face so many anxieties and pressures surrounding school and work. Depression hits me hard sometimes too, and it's hard to feel different from everyone else around me.

I know that the right answer is to have trust in God and to know that he is good. Sometimes I just want you to validate that what I am feeling is hard and is hurtful. I want to hear from you that I am strong and that I am doing good and that my feelings do matter. Don't brush them off.

I love you, but don't smother me. I need boundaries, but I feel like if I tell you that it will hurt you. I don't want to hurt you; I never want to hurt you. So I don't tell you these things all the time.

Mom, I'm not as confident as I can sometimes come off as being. I have many insecurities that I don't know what to do about, and I wish we were closer sometimes. It feels like you are not around enough to get to the place in our relationship where I feel like I can tell you these things.

I wish I was able to talk to you. I feel that you will judge me or get mad at me whenever I tell you anything. Some of the things I feel are key to why we fight. I would love to share with you without fear of your reactions. I love you to death, Mom, but sometimes I don't feel comfortable telling you things.

Thank you, Mom, for giving me a safe place to share.

Mom writes:

Dear Daughter,

Thank you for sharing your heart with me. I am so proud of you, I love you, and with God's help I promise I am going to take to heart everything you share with me. My girl, is there anything I say or do that makes you feel worse about yourself or the way that you look? It is never my intention to make you feel this way, but we all make mistakes. I want to learn how I can be better for you.

Daughter writes:

Dear Mom,

I know it's not intentional, but when you put yourself or your body down it makes me question mine since we have a similar build. I love you so much, and I hate hearing you talk negatively about yourself. It makes me feel like I always have to be fit. Even through all the seasons of my body changing, I look back and wish I didn't spend so much time worrying about working out or getting fit.

And because you are so beautiful, I feel like I have high standards to meet.

It makes me so upset when you make comments about my weight or compare me to other people's sizes. Or when every time I see you, I feel like you look me up and down. Or when you ask me things like "How much do you weigh?" "How much weight have you gained or lost?" Or when we look through magazines to order clothes and you say to me, "Oh, honey, I'm sorry but that doesn't come in chubby size."

I feel sometimes like I don't get to make my own choices about my clothes or hair. I take offense when you tell me my hair doesn't look right or that something I am wearing might be inappropriate. For example, when we go shopping, I hate having to buy shorts. Even if it is hot! I wish you understood that I dread wearing them because I think they make me look bigger than I am. I wish I had known how to explain to you how much I hated that.

It makes me feel worse when you comment about my food choices or judge me when I am relaxing for the day. At first when you said things about what I ate, I think it didn't bother me. But recently I began to struggle again with an eating disorder, and I realized I cannot get your words out of my head.

Mom, I know you love me, but sometimes it feels like you have a hard time complimenting me, and when you yell it makes me feel like I am not important or special.

I love you so much, Mom. There are so many things about you that I love. Thank you for giving me the time to talk a little about the things that hurt. It feels good to get them out.

Mom writes:

Dear Daughter,

I always want to hear about all the things on your mind! I am sorry if I have not been there to listen to them before, but I am here now. I am listening, I am learning, and I am ready. Sweet girl, how can I model confidence for you? What can I do that will help you remember that you are valued, special, and created beautiful just the way you are?

Daughter writes:

Dear Mom,

I love when you text me randomly and tell me you love me. I love how you tell me I look cute when I get dressed up or when I am just looking lazy at home. I love when you tell me I am loved, that I am pretty, and that you are proud of me. I love how you tell me I am amazing, and I know that you mean it!

I love how you love people well. You fight for me at school, and I know you always have my back. You are a positive person; you believe every person is good. You are my biggest cheerleader, and you always tell me I am doing great! It might be for the silliest things, but when you tell me that you are proud of me I love that I believe you. There is something about me that will always want your approval.

I love when you tell me that you saw something that reminded you of me, and then you get it for me because it made you think of me. I love that! I know you think I am the most special kid on the planet, and I can feel your confidence in me.

I love when you tell me I look nice and you take the time to compliment my achievements.

I love how you wear your hair out and wild; you have always been so beautiful in my eyes. Your style is so great, and I love how you have never been afraid to be yourself. I love when you dress up in fancy attire and go all out with your makeup. So fun.

I love your "just because" notes, and our mom and daughter shopping or spa days are the best!

I love when you remind me to be myself and not punish myself by wearing clothes that don't feel comfortable on my body.

I love that you remind me who I am and that my value is in Christ. You encourage me to carry myself like a lady with grace and confidence. I love that you help me choose clothes that suit my personality and body type. They are always tasteful and make me feel confident and beautiful. I have noticed that choosing clothes that fit well helps me not to be so self-aware and discontent with my body shape.

Thank you for taking extra time to spend with me; I feel so loved when we are together just the two of us. I love how you always do special things for us around the holidays and our birthdays. You always go above and beyond!

You are a strong woman; you are positive, optimistic, and encouraging. Your encouragement is deep and profound, and you model to me by being yourself, taking care of yourself, loving yourself, and never speaking poorly of who you are.

Mom, I think you are amazing in so many ways.

Mom writes:

Dear Daughter,

It has been such a blessing to hear from you. You have given me a lot to think about and pray about. I know that together and with God's help, you and I can be confident women. How do you think we can have a positive impact on those around us? You know, make people be more confident and love the body they are in?

Daughter writes:

Dear Mom,

I think we can start by not judging. We should compliment people on the way they look. We can be positive and kind, and we can smile.

We can call out their beauty, because all girls are beautiful. Giving small words of encouragement goes a long way; it's taking the time to notice little things and then telling that person. Everyone wants to feel special and loved. We can give words of encouragement; a simple compliment can go a long way for boosting confidence and body image.

We can stress the point that if you love yourself, then you are enough for everyone else too. As teens, we ask ourselves, "Am I cool enough, pretty enough, or smart enough?" I used to ask myself this a lot, but once I started to love myself more, things got clearer. We can steer clear of those questions. We can try to stop striving for perfection. I think it helps when we are willing to show one another our flaws and find new ways to let one another know that we all share a similar struggle.

We can stop comparing ourselves to one another all the time. Women uplifting other women comes in so many forms. Pointing out unique strengths in another person makes them feel loved and valued. It also helps me take the focus off myself and try to be more thoughtful to others.

We can write the words God believes about us over our hearts. When we feel defenseless against the words of the world, we know his words are the ones of our true worth.

Mom writes:

Dear Daughter,

You are so wise. If it's okay, I am going to pray for you now. No, I am going to pray for us. I hope that you fold this prayer up and keep it in a safe place. Open it and read it when you need it most, and you can always remember how much I love you, how much God loves you, and how much we are in this together.

An End and a Beginning

Welcome to the first day of forever.

From now on, I pray you will not see the world the same. Sure, sometimes it will make you come off like a crazy woman when you give random people in public a death stare at the mention of the words *diet*, *fat*, or *ugly* around your children. It's okay, you are in good company. We are in this thing together. Confident moms and confident daughters are meant to stick together.

It might be a little uncomfortable at first, as we stand up tall in our confidence while the world mutters around us in a constant battle for *better* or *more*. But us? Our girls? We are already whole. With Christ in us, there is no greater form of beauty we can achieve.

I pray grace over you, my sister, my fellow momma, and my Proverbs 31 friend, and I want you to know that with every keystroke I prayed for *you* and *your amazing daughter*. Though our journey ends here, may we stay strong and true to the truth God revealed to us and may we stand shoulder to shoulder in *his* perfect confidence.

Confident Mom
CHALLENGE

Challenge #12: All right, Momma, it's your turn! You got this. Write letters back and forth with your daughter. If you have to resort to bribery in order to get her to respond, do it. You don't have to feel the need to ask probing questions or go deep, but open up the door for her to share in the safety of paper and pen. Aim for four exchanges, pray every time before you write, and let the Holy Spirit guide the discussion. Your last letter to her can be in the form of a prayer over her that she can hold on to, but you make the rules here.

Bonus Challenge: Make a date to sit down with her and go through the discussion questions below (these are the same questions I posed in the Confidence Survey). I suggest prepping her for this one, so she knows it is going to be a deep dive, and asking her to come prepared to share. Mom, you come prepared to share too about your relationship with your mom. You are at the graduate level of confidence now that you have made it this far. You can do this!

Confident Daughter
DISCUSSION QUESTIONS

1. What is something you wish your mom (or daughter) knew, but you never had the courage before now to tell her?

2. Is there anything that your mom (or daughter) does that makes you feel worse about yourself or the way you look?

3. What are some ways that your mom (or daughter) models confidence for you? What things make you feel special, valued, and created beautiful just the way you are?

4. What are some ways that you think women can have a positive impact on your confidence and your body image?

5. Let's talk about healing. Are there any hurts that have been mentioned in this conversation that you would like to ask your mom's (or your daughter's) forgiveness for?

6. Moving forward, what would you like to work on in your relationship with your mom (or daughter)?

7. Have there been any areas of broken trust? Can you name them? Can you offer forgiveness?

8. Tomorrow is a new day, a fresh start. Name some things that, moving forward, you want to try not to dwell on anymore.

9. What are some things that, moving forward, you want to try to start dwelling on more?

10. Can you be brave together? Can you take a moment to pray for each other? If you feel nervous praying out loud, grab a pen and paper and write out your prayer instead.

A Mom's Prayer

Dear God, thank you for this opportunity to hear honestly from my daughter. I ask for your forgiveness for any of the ways I may have made her struggles harder through the years. You know that was never my intention. But I praise you because you are a God of hope and you are a God of healing, and my daughter and I do not need to look backward. We pray only to move forward with you. I ask that you bring healing to any places of hurt between the two of us and that in the place of the hurt you create new life in us. I pray that my relationship with my daughter would be special, one in which together we can grow, learn, and become the confident women we desire to be. Lord, help me to be strong for her! I confess to you that I will never have it all figured out, but I am sitting with you here asking for your wisdom. Help me to show her the way to you. Help me to pave a way that shows her that loving our body is possible, that being confident is possible, and that we do not need to stay chained to our feelings of insecurity, inadequacy, and never being enough. You are a God of miracles. I believe that you are the same yesterday, today, and forever, and we are asking for the miracle of being at peace in our imperfections. Hand in hand with my daughter, I pray you would help our striving to cease and that we would be able to sit still in joyful contentment. You know that the battles of this life will be many—we will not be out of the woods until we meet you again—but I pray that from here on out my daughter and I will be in this battle together, arm in arm. Would you help the battles against each other to cease and our time for peace to be now? Thank you for my daughter! Thank you for her beauty, her character, her courage, her wisdom, her kindness, her passion. You are so good to have given her to me. I ask that you go with her now, that this day your Holy Spirit would prove to her beyond a shadow of a doubt that you are good, you are powerful, and you are here. Amen!

Confident Moms, Confident Daughters
MANIFESTO
Based on Proverbs 31

I am beautiful because I have character.

I am beautiful because I know that my character is worth more than all the money in the world.

I am beautiful because I am confident.

I am beautiful because I find joy in putting others above myself.

I am beautiful because I work hard.

I am beautiful because I seek to provide for those around me.

I am beautiful because I love to learn new things.

I am beautiful because I use my body for what it is meant for—work of all kinds.

I am beautiful because I get the job done.

I am beautiful because I am generous.

I am beautiful because I do not fear my future, not because I know it will all go perfectly but because I know that God will be there.

I am beautiful because I choose company with other women of strong character.

I am beautiful because I am responsible.

I am beautiful because I am strong.

I am beautiful because I have dignity.

I am beautiful because I laugh.

I am beautiful because I speak wisdom.

I am beautiful because I receive praise with grace and humility.

I am beautiful because I am noble.

I am beautiful because I know that physical beauty fades and you won't catch me putting my value in looks.

I am beautiful because I trust the Lord above all else.

I am beautiful because I am God's daughter.

Acknowledgments

To my beautiful family, thank you. Dave, Faith, David, Aaron, and Sammy, you have been so patient with all of Mommy's writing things. You send me off with joy, prayer, and encouragement, and it brings me such peace. Thank you for loving me just as I am. I love you soooo much.

To my Faith. It is for you that this book was written. I pray that someday you might come to understand the full impact that your life has had on me and so many others. You were my motivation to finally be better, be stronger, and be confident. Thank you, sweet girl. I love you forever and always.

To my Dave. You are the best editor and supporter in the whole wide world. I would not be anywhere without your constant encouragement and your impeccable editing skills. Thank you for letting me do all that God has called me to. I love you.

To my mom and dad. I am positive that this book isn't always easy to read. Thank you for giving me the freedom, the permission, and the encouragement to share anything that God lay on my heart to share. Mom, thank you for being such a willing learner; you give me the space to share with you without ever making me feel guilty. It is a gift you have given me. I love you both. (And Nick, you're okay too.)

To Andrea Doering and Chip MacGregor. You were the very first two people to spur me on in this project. Thank you for your confidence in me and the message of this book. I have immense respect for the way you both go about your work, and I have learned so much from your wisdom and experience. Thank you for allowing me the space to do what I feel called to do and in the way that is most honoring to who I am.

To Jennifer Dukes Lee. Thank you so much for your quick "yes" to writing the foreword. You have a gift for words and an even greater gift for lifting up our Savior, and I am ever grateful to God for putting you in my life. You have set a beautiful example for me as a writer, and I admire you deeply. Thank you!

To all of my beautiful and talented writer friends. It is such an honor and a joy getting to walk this life with you. Being a writer can lay you bare, but having you as friends to learn from and vent to has made it survivable and (mostly) enjoyable. Marissa Henley, Meredith McDaniel, Adriel McIntosh Booker, Niki Hardy, Alicia Bruxvoort, Tracy Steel, and Myquillyn Smith—thank you!

To so many dear family and friends who patiently endure me as I write: my sisters, Bre DeBeauvernet, Nancy Bolinger, Jenny Goddard, and Rachel Furlough, and all the rest of the fam; my friends Greta Jones, Cammie Howard, Ashley Walker, Kim Muhich, Melissa Alvarez, and Amy Crossan; and my discipleship ladies, Stefanie, Amanda, Lauran, Laura, Becky, Jen, Lindsay, and Kristi. Thank you for standing by me, supporting me, praying for me, and loving me even when I disappear for months at a time.

To Karrie Dobie. Thank you so much for being willing to partner with me and help me with all my "crazy." You help keep me sane.

To Carrie Sumner. Girl, I believe God plopped you into my life to show me exactly what he means by *confident*. Thank you for being constant and unwavering you.

To Lindsey Laszewski and Emily Kearney-Begg. Thank you, thank you for showing me what a confident mom and confident daughter look like. Thank you for not knowing what it means to calorie count, for walk-clapping with me, and for giving me hope that there is a different way to be.

To Dr. Kymberly Selden, Quinn Foley, Angela Wilkinson, Lauran Harmon, Meredith McDaniel, Kristen Hatton, Carrie Sumner, Taylor Howard, Chris DeBeauvernet, and all the anonymous beautiful women who took the Confidence Survey. I believe that the best part of this book is your contributions. Gathering advice, wisdom, and experience from you has made this book wonderful. Thank you!

To my Black Rock family. Over ten years ago, Black Rock Church in Fairfield, Connecticut, took a chance on a right-out-of-college twenty-something-year-old. They gave me a full-time job in youth ministry that ignited a fire in me that has never gone out. Thank you for trusting me to love on your amazing children. And to my Club JVers and Fusioners, I will love you always. This book, in many ways, exists because of you. Kevin and Kerrie Butterfield, you invested in and mentored me in a way that has permanently impacted me. Thank you for introducing me to Jesus and all the wisdom and gifts that come with knowing him.

To my Lake Forest family, especially all my women's ministry friends. You keep me going! I don't think I would make it through much of anything if not for you.

To my amazing endorsers: Gwen Smith, Alicia Bruxvoort, Kate Battistelli, Amanda Bacon, Cheri Gregory, and Lori Benham. You have been true friends to me in this writing process, and I am so grateful for your partnership in this ministry. And, most of all, thank you for being Confident Moms for your Girls!

To all of my sisterly HopeWriter author friends. You bring me so much joy and laughter.

To so many of you at Revell. I am grateful for you daily. Thank you, Erin Smith, Erin Bartels, Patti Brinks, Brianne Dekker, Gisèle Mix, and Abby Van Wormer.

Notes

Chapter 1 Showing Her Confident

1. Claire Shipman and Cole Kazdin, "Teens: Oral Sex and Casual Prostitution No Biggie," *ABC News*, May 28, 2009, http://abcnews.go.com/GMA/Parenting /story?id=7693121&page=1.

2. Mayo Clinic Staff, "Self-Injury/Cutting," Mayo Clinic, December 7, 2018, http://www.mayoclinic.com/health/self-injury/DS00775.

Chapter 3 If We Don't, Then Who Will?

1. Walt Mueller, "In Particular," Center for Parent/Youth Understanding, 2006, https://cpyu.org/resource/in-particular/.

2. Pamela Haag, *Voices of a Generation: Teenage Girls on Sex, School, and Self* (Washington, DC: American Association of University Women, 1999), 9.

Chapter 5 A Moment on the Lips

1. "Teen Brain: Behavior, Problem Solving, and Decision Making," Facts for Families, no. 95 (September 2016), American Academy of Child and Adolescent Psychiatry, https://www.aacap.org/aacap/families_and_youth/facts_for_families /FFF-Guide/The-Teen-Brain-Behavior-Problem-Solving-and-Decision-Making -095.aspx.

Chapter 6 Let's Get Physical

1. "Dieting in Adolescence," *Pediatrics & Child Health* 9, no. 7 (September 2004): 487–91, https://www.ncbi.nlm.nih.gov/pmc/articles/PMC2720870/.

2. J. Vernon McGee, *Thru the Bible with J. Vernon McGee*, vol. 5 (Nashville: Thomas Nelson, 1983), 448–49.

3. Merriam-Webster, s.v. "training," https://www.merriam-webster.com/diction ary/training.

Chapter 7 Sticks and Stones

1. Henry Cloud, *Integrity: The Courage to Meet the Demands of Reality* (New York: HarperCollins, 2006), 66–67.

Chapter 10 Our Jesus and Our Joy

1. Jennifer Dukes Lee, *The Happiness Dare* (Carol Stream, IL: Tyndale, 2016), 31, emphasis original.

Maria Furlough is a wife to one awesome husband, Dave, who is half editor, half cheerleader, half hilarious, and half amazing. She is a mother to one amazing eleven-year-old daughter, three ridiculously fun boys, and one baby boy who lives in the arms of Jesus. She works at Lake Forest Church in Huntersville, North Carolina, teaches women's Bible studies, and is a former full-time youth pastor. The author of *Breaking the Fear Cycle*, Maria currently blogs at www.mariafurlough.com.

Connect with Maria!

Visit **MariaFurlough.com**
for **FREE** downloadable resources for
Confident Moms, Confident Daughters

#ConfidentMomsandDaughters

Maria.Furlough

MariaFurlough

MariaFurloughAuthor@gmail.com

Overcome Fear for Good

How *to*
Find Peace
for Your
Anxious
Heart

*breaking the
fear cycle*

Maria Furlough

Using her own story as a catalyst, Maria Furlough discusses how to overcome fear for good. With practicality and passion, she shows us the steps we can take to bring those fears to God rather than act on them and to trust God with the future.

LET'S TALK ABOUT BOOKS

- Share or mention the book on your social media platforms. Use the hashtag **#ConfidentMomsandDaughters**.

- Write a book review on your blog or on a retailer site.

- Pick up a copy for friends, family, or anyone who you think would enjoy and be challenged by its message!

- Share this message on Twitter, Facebook, or Instagram: **I loved #ConfidentMomsandDaughters by @MariaFurlough // @RevellBooks**

- Recommend this book for your church, workplace, book club, or small group.

- Follow Revell on social media and tell us what you like.

 RevellBooks

 RevellBooks

 RevellBooks